Praise from Advance Readers and Workshop Participants

It stirred so many memories with good pacing and gentle persistence. It works and it helps.
> *—Eric Greenleaf, Ph.D.*

So simple and completely natural that everybody ought to know how to do it. It's invaluable for a person who wants to write anything, using his own past as material. Whenever personal experience and memories are involved, this would be extremely useful.
> *—Richard Olney, developer of*
> *Self-Acceptance Training*

....a very subtle and gentle technique for recapturing memories of childhood, and thereby enriching one's life. It will be useful to those who wish to reestablish a closer bond to their younger years (by filling in memory gaps of early relationships and events), as well as to those who are searching for additional self-awareness, and finally to writers who would find a fuller range of memories useful in their work.
> *—Russell Lee, M.D., Psychiatrist*

We appreciated your humor, your command of the material and your gentle way of presenting the material. As a team we felt that the memories we retrieved helped us remember our pasts in a way that felt enriching and safe. We want to do more.
> *—Peter H. Cole, LCSW, Clinical Instructor of Psychiatry,*
> *University of California, Davis School of Medicine*

The method is not only fascinating but fun. Perhaps one day we will bring our children and grandchildren into intergenerational workshops, so we can all understand each other's experiences better.
> *—Martin Lichterman, Ph.D., professor emeritus of history*
> *and board member, Alternative Lifelong Learning*

Wendlinger uses his own experiences to illustrate the exercises, providing a rich legacy for his own children and for others who wish to meet him in a deeper way. This models the concept for parents and families who want to introduce themselves to each other in different ways than they have in the past. An original and effective resource!
> *—Marcia Perlstein, MFCC*

Our memories have already added zest to our marriage. Now I'm planning to use triggering techniques with my mother to get a better grasp of my family history.
> *—Participant in a memory triggering workshop at a*
> *national conference of the National Association of*
> *Social Workers*

One Person's Memory Triggering Experience

Tape-recorded a few hours after a memory triggering workshop:

"As soon as I got the idea of your memory maps, I was simply astounded.

"Here's a spot where I had a fist fight with a kid when I was eight years old, my first fight. Here's another where I watched my cousin, who was my idol, three years older than I, fighting with a kid who was much bigger than he was.

"Here's where I was walking home from school with my 12-year-old aunt, like my older sister, only six years older than I was. And when the snow started to fall, she caught a flake on her coat and looked at it very closely and told us that they were six-pointed and no two were ever alike, which was an incredible piece of learning for me.

"The memories are so vivid. I can see my young aunt with her normally pale face all glowing red and white. And the brilliant red of her wool coat. She had a coat that—well—I couldn't begin to describe it. I'm being carried away, as you can see. I'm right there, right this minute. And this was true of one thing after the other.

"The one and only time that I ever skipped grammar school, when I came home and expected to be welcomed by my mother—I think with a sandwich or something—instead she raised the devil with me.

"And when I had to wear a new green sweater that I despised. Because my mother had bought it for me and my father insisted that I wear it to school. And how I stood in the doorway of the school and wouldn't play with the kids because I was wearing this sweater. I can just go on and on.

"You see what's happening? Several hours after doing the map, just remembering what my map is like is still carrying me along. This method is really exciting.

"It's amazing. Even while I'm talking about this with you, I'm back there again, back in my childhood. It's really taking me back. It gave me a feeling of being surrounded by open air and sunshine even though I was sitting in this stuffy seminar room when we did it. It's like we're feeling here, in this hot humidity, and then feeling this breeze, and how good it feels. It has the same sense!"

—Richard Olney, Developer of Self-Acceptance Training, at Ixtapa, Mexico, December 1991

THE MEMORY TRIGGERING BOOK

Using Your Memories to
Enhance Your Life and Your Relationships

Robert M. Wendlinger

PROUST PRESS

Berkeley, California

For more information and orders, contact:

Proust Press
6239 College Ave., #303
Oakland, CA 94618
Telephone 510-845-5551
CompuServe: 73151,1702

Wendlinger, Robert M.
The Memory Triggering Book: Using Your Memories to Enhance Your Life and Your Relationships — 1st ed.
205 pages. Reading list.

1. Memory—autobiographical memory, process of remembering
2. Writing—memoirs, autobiography, journals
3. Psychology—creativity, self-help, relationships
4. Creativity—unblocking memories
5. Gerontology—life review and reminiscence programs

Design and Production: Watermark Design Group
Creative Director: Tara Eglin
Photography: Barbara Sonnenborn
Typeset in Adobe Garamond and Stone Sans
Printed and bound by McNaughton & Gunn Inc., Saline, MI

To Joan

My Lover, My Teacher, My Friend, My Wife,

The Best

Contents

The Memory Triggering Book

The Exercises 49

Epilogue

Appendix

Exhibits

Story Triggers

Mini-Memories

If I knew things would no longer be, I would have tried to remember better.

THE FATHER, in Barry Levinson's film, *Avalon* (1990)

The past is hidden...in some material object...which we do not suspect....it depends on chance whether we come upon it or not....

....the smell and taste of things remain poised a long time, like souls, ready to remind us, waiting and hoping for their moment, [of] the vast structure of recollection.

MARCEL PROUST
Remembrance of Things Past

Memory is a blessing; it creates bonds rather than destroys them. It provides the opportunity to redeem one's past and link to the future.

ELIE WEISEL

Foreword

By Miriam Polster, Ph.D. & Erving R. Polster, Ph.D. Directors, Gestalt Institute of San Diego-California

Most of us stand, like children with hands outstretched, projecting forward into the future but still clasping whatever we can remember from our past. And thus our future is *cantilevered* from the past; to the extent we remember richly, our personal cantilevers seem solid and we feel well situated in the world. Indeed, our present experience gains dimension and resonance when we can discern in it traces of the people, places, and sensations that left their mark on us and incline us to be the individuals we presently are.

Much recent memory work has seemed to specialize in recalling scenes and relationships of trauma and hurt. But there is more to be remembered than childhood trauma. Although a certain memory may have elements of regret, sadness, or shame, it may–in the perspective of time elapsed–also move us forward into forgiveness, sympathy, understanding. We may also discover acknowledgement, a sense of evolution, and the illumination of new aspects of ourselves and our personalities that we have perhaps overlooked or undervalued. We can reestablish a sense of connection between memorable people and influences in our lives and may consequently move into a contemporary awareness of our own impact and potential contribution to the lives of our families, friends, and communities.

With his dynamic concept of "triggers," Bob Wendlinger invites us to reclaim memories of our past, and demonstrates how to make them register sharply, rich in detail. His instructions are specific and carefully conceived entries into past experience. Wendlinger uses all the senses–smell and taste and vision and hearing and even touch–as avenues for recovering the ingredients of memory.

I'm amazed, over and over again, at how fascinating people are even though they start out either boring or thinking they are boring. The stories they tell are just beyond ordinary belief. This particular man...you could almost cry hearing his story; and in the beginning, nothing.

—ERVING POLSTER, Ph.D., *psychotherapist*

Furthermore, his instructions are developed in a sequence that permits moving flexibly from one subset of memories–for example, the key events in one's life–that may then in turn illuminate a new aspect of a previous subset. As Wendlinger shows, this can be a productive way of putting together previous glimpses of a life and finding new sense in them.

For most of us, clinical amnesia is a frightening prospect, severing people from their pasts and leaving them somewhat like victims of a psychological amputation. In the hurly-burly of everyday responsibilities, we all suffer a sort of self-imposed amnesia, perhaps the best alternative we could come up with at the moment, but now-and-then seeming meager or less colorful than we would like. As this book shows, memories can also enrich, hearten and inspire.

Bob Wendlinger has given us a guide book to go back in personal time and fill in some of the blanks. We emerge knowing ourselves better and feeling–yes–more *whole*.

Miriam and Erving Polster are leading teachers of Gestalt therapy internationally and co-authors of *Gestalt Therapy Integrated* (Brunner/Mazel). Miriam Polster has also written *Eve's Daughters: The Forbidden Heroism of Women* (Jossey-Bass), and Erving Polster is author of *Population of Selves: Therapeutic Explorations of Personal Diversity* (Jossey-Bass) and *Every Person's Life is Worth a Novel* (Norton).

VISTING A RELATIVE OUT OF TOWN

DRIVING CROSSCOUNTRY WITH YO

THE SOUND OF A FOGHORN

ABOUT MEMORY TRIGGERING

SINGING SONGS AROUND A CAMPFIRE

THE SMELL OF FRESH APPLE PIE

FLYING A KITE ON A WINDY DAY

Memory Triggering Can Improve Your Life

Memory triggering is a process to help you remember the details and textures of your life, and then *apply* your memories in ways that will enhance your life *right now*. You will remember your *autobiographical* memories, going as far back as early childhood but not restricted to that period of life.

It has been tested over a period of more than ten years, first on myself, then on friends and family, and finally in various workshops and individual sessions with people of all ages and interests, including social workers, psychologists and writers. All provided valuable feedback, corrections, and validation.

Memory triggering can be a pleasant and informative way to remember–in the midst of pressures of everyday life –who you have been and what you have accomplished over time. It can also be a vehicle for remembering and healing the more difficult aspects of a life, including regret, sadness, and shame. So for many people, memory triggering is about *exploring* the memories that are triggered, and using them in various ways to improve the quality of their lives in the here-and-now.

Your own goals for these explorations can be as modest or as ambitious as you like. Some have been satisfied to use these techniques for a few hours of casual play, while others have used their new memories to provide the opportunity for another jump start in life, or to enliven a new or long-term relationship, or to *unblock*–through powerful memories–an important creative project.

The Triggering Experience

The triggering experience itself is familiar to most of us:

- Marj walks down an unfamiliar country road at dusk; she is triggered by the odors and the quality of

....*suddenly the memory returns. The taste [the trigger] was that of the little crumb of madeleine which on Sunday mornings at Combray.... my Aunt Leonie used to give me, dipping it first in her own cup of real or of lime-flower tea...*

—MARCEL PROUST
*Remembrance of
Things Past*

*S.'s memory trigger: Smelling
a favorite flower of her
adolescent years*

light into memories of her summer camp two decades ago.

- Roz smells her daughter's gardenia and is triggered into memories of her own high school prom.

- Bill holds his son's new football, brings it to his nose, and remembers his own experience trying out for his high school team–and not making it.

Triggers–yours and mine–will often be different. Or are you triggered, as I am, into Army memories by the steamy odor of any ship's galley? Even when our triggers are identical, our memories will be different. Mother and daughter: the same triggering flower, but memories of two different experiences with different people at different times. So triggering tends to accentuate our distinctiveness and the uniqueness of our experience.

When such memories occur, we realize that this is not our ordinary experience of remembering voluntarily. In some way our senses have recovered the special quality of our early lives–the feeling, the color, and the atmosphere–that cannot be recovered when we attempt with words and concepts to recall our pasts. (In this way, memory triggering can be significantly different from the techniques of oral history and similar techniques.)

Sometimes my triggers may seem unusual to you, and yours to me. A particular favorite of mine is the smell of melted tar in the process of road repair, a scent that evokes the loveliest neighborhood memories for me! Some of your triggers will leave me unaffected, particularly if you grew up on a farm, for I have no experience of rural life.

You should know that this entire book is capable of triggering your memories, not merely the section called "The Workbook." So even before you begin to use the workbook, you will find that ruled lines are included within the wide margins on most pages. You can use

them for quickly jotting down the key words of your memories immediately after they are triggered–and before you forget them. (You may prefer to use a notepad or another means of capturing your memories; more about this later.)

Perhaps you have already remembered favorite triggers or memories of yours. If you have, capture then now, perhaps in the wide margins of this book.

Some Definitions

The process of remembering is called triggering, and the techniques and cues that stimulate memories to appear are called triggers. Some of the techniques were my own inventions; others, like the use of sensory triggers, were suggested to me by the work of Marcel Proust and others, including recent studies by various memory researchers.

Typical triggering techniques are the memory maps, floor plans, lists, questions, and activities you will find in the book. These will be effective with most everyone.

Your personal triggers can be anything that has the ability to stimulate a memory of your particular life experience: a certain sound, smell, taste, feeling, word, person, event, concept, dream, fantasy, object, picture, visit, reunion, question, movie, thought, activity. Especially, another memory. This book will help you to identify those personal triggers unique to your life–for example, a particular song or scent–that can help you recall important life experiences.

The Uses of Triggering

Triggering is for those of any age who respect their memories, find pleasure and knowledge in remembering, and want to *engage* with their memories toward some form of self-discovery or other creative work: journal-writing,

The dispersion and reconstitution of the self. That's the whole story.

—BAUDELAIRE
My Heart Laid Bare

B.'s memory trigger: Exploring the family photo album (Bobby, Moodus, CT, 1930s)

painting, acting, or the like. Users could include a young person fascinated by nostalgic products or by the music of his parents; a middle-aged woman encouraging her husband to share more of his early history with her; an older man who wants to leave a permanent record of his life as a legacy for his grandchildren; or a family that likes to get together to explore stories of their ancestors and their history.

Together with the joys and pleasures, the users of triggering will also learn from the bittersweet and sometimes painful feelings that may sometimes emerge when remembering.

In my workshops and individual counseling, the users of triggering seem to fall into four main groups:

- **Self-Explorers** want to learn more about the people and events of their past to help them live more fully and deeply in the present. Their memories help them understand why they behave and interact with others as they do. They are interested in possibilities for significant life changes, and in sharing themselves more intimately with others who are important to them.

- **Memory Workers** trigger memories to provide material for their creative work. This group includes fiction writers, both published and unpublished, painters, sculptors, method actors, clients in psychotherapy, and even young students of English composition. Triggering can be particularly useful to those with creative "blocks."

- **Connectors** trigger memories to share them with their partners, children or parents, to strengthen their family ties and their ethnic roots, and perhaps to pass along a written or audio-visual record of their memories to their descendants, much as their ancestors passed "oral histories" from one generation to another.

- **Past-Times Travellers** are drawn toward warm nostalgia, and remembrances of people, places, and events from the past, including celebrities of music, films, and sports that still have meaning and significance for them in the here-and-now.

Do you seem to fit into any of these groups? If you're not certain what use you would make of triggering and new memories, you might study the list of questions on page 24.

How the Triggering Method was Developed

I am an editor, writer, and teacher. I began to work seriously on the triggering method after my realization, some five years after my father's death, that I could not remember a single conversation that the two of us had ever had. I knew little about his personal history, his values, or his state of mind at any particular time in his life. And I was angry and I felt cheated.

At the time, I had been recently divorced, feeling guilty about the pain I had caused my three children, and (as I understood later) fearful of losing their love and being as unknown to them at my death as my father had been to me. So I decided that, as their legacy from me, they would have as complete and as accurate a record of *my* life as I could remember, and they could use it (or not use it) at any time, any way they wished. They could read it, talk about it with each other or with me, ignore it until after I had died, or ignore it forever (not a chance). But this gift would be theirs, and the way they used it would be their choice.

There was a problem, however. I couldn't remember my life very well. And I needed some techniques to help stimulate the details that I hoped to share. I had some hints from my own experience as a writing teacher and from memory research, about how I might access these

Creativity is the act of bringing something new into the world, whether a symphony, a novel, a supermarket or a new casserole. It is based on communication with oneself, then testing that communication with experience and reality.

—S.I. HAYAKAWA

A.'s memory trigger: Eating his very special childhood treat

memories, and create a process for recapturing a life. And of course the memory world of Marcel Proust fascinated me, as it has bewitched many writers who longed for a similar experience: here was a man who (apparently) slipped into an eight-volume masterpiece of memory recall after tasting and smelling–decades after the first experience–a crumb of a particular French cookie dipped in lime tea!

So I began to develop a method for remembering myself, applying and refining the techniques as I went along, discovering the particular smells, tastes, and music that triggered my memories. I created my own techniques, like the mapping exercises you will find in this book, testing them first on family and friends, and later in large workshops.

In time, I had several hundred stories about my life that I could present to my children. (Some are included in the book.) When woven together these snapshots tell me (and others) who I was at different times of my life and who I am now, particularly when others can ask me to elaborate on them.

And something happened that I had not expected or sought. As I remembered myself, I triggered long-forgotten episodes involving my father as well, and he became more alive and real to me! This was triggering's unanticipated gift to me! Your gifts to yourself will be different, I am sure, but I hope no less important and no less rewarding. Good luck with whatever you choose to do with the triggering techniques!

Setting Your Personal Goals

Do you need a goal before beginning to trigger your memories? Some people are uncomfortable beginning any project without a clear direction; they will want to relate triggering to a specific goal or project. Others may prefer to begin from a position of simple curiosity, or with the expectation of being entertained or educated, and wait to see what will happen. The triggering process does not require that you choose one way or another.

Experience tells us that memories can have many different uses at different periods in our lives; in no particular order of importance, they may become material for:

- *creative projects* (journals, memoirs, family legacies, school compositions, and fiction);

- programs of *self-development*, self-conducted or with the help of others;

- stories for *pleasurable reminiscing* and *deepened relationships* with partners and families;

- *games and entertainments* within groups of family and friends;

- *opportunities* for resolving conflicts and giving more meaning to one's life.

Whether or not you begin triggering with a specific goal or outcome in mind, it's likely that your memories themselves will suggest what should be done with them: one memory is so lovely and charming that it demands to be shared with someone; a second is too difficult or painful to share; a third seems so important that you want to add it immediately to your journal or your family writing project.

My experience, as I conducted triggering sessions with groups and individuals, is that some will have goals that are clearly articulated: "There's something in my life that's troubling me. Maybe this will give me some ideas on how to deal with it."

Others may have no more than a sense or intuition that their memories could be beneficial or interesting in some way, and proceed from there.

I found that the most crucial problems of relationship stemmed most often from "not telling."....Do you not know that words are eggs, that words carry life, that words are eggs?

—RUSSELL
LOCKHART
Words as Eggs

*L.'s memory trigger:
Smelling mother's perfume.*

And of course your goals may change as you move through the triggering process, sometimes without your knowledge, as mine did. Sometime the shift will be subtle and inconspicuous; at other times, glaring and clear. I began this project to remember more about myself and to share that new part of myself with my children, and I "ended" (for now, that is) finding my father instead.

At every step of the triggering process, you can use your understanding of what you want from life at that moment, so that whatever you do with your memories would flow in an organic way from the memories themselves.

Discover your own way of applying your memories to your life—and use them as simply, deeply, wisely, foolishly, or frivolously as you choose. Whatever you do will be a challenge to your creativity: to your ability to make new connections–between past and present, among feelings, thoughts and actions–that can enhance the quality of your life.

Questions About Your Personal Triggering Goals

Here are ten questions I ask at the beginning of my memory triggering workshops. Answer them if you're not yet certain about your specific goals for triggering, and if you need to have a goal before proceeding. All can be answered "Yes" or "No." For a more precise rating, use a scale of "1" to "10"–"1" being the strongest "No" possible and "10" being the most positive "Yes."

- If you're a creative professional or are ambitious to be a writer, artist, or actor: Would you like to have more creative energy and perhaps use your personal memories as material in your work?

- Can you anticipate exchanging newly remembered memories with important people in your life–partners, friends, parents, other family–to be closer to them, and to enliven new relationships as well?

- Would you like to create your "life review" as a legacy to your family and grandchildren, perhaps focus on your cultural or ethnic background, so they might know you better right now, and remember you more fully later?

- Do you enjoy being nostalgic and remembering the past, because life in some ways seemed more pleasurable then?

- Would you like to understand–for your enlightenment or entertainment–how the episodes, places and people of your earlier years helped to shape your future?

- Would you like to use your early memories in some form of personal writing—journals, memoirs, autobiography, or essays?

- If you're a student at any level of school: Would you prefer to write compositions about your deeply felt personal memories than about subjects assigned by a teacher?

- Would you like to explore what makes you special and unique as a person—since the specific details and texture of your life-experience have been unlike anyone else's?

- What other purpose not yet mentioned might you have for accessing more memories of your life?

How This Book is Organized

- **Part One. About Memory Triggering**. After this brief introductory section are two stories that demonstrate how triggered memories can be applied to improve a couple's relationship—in this case, my wife's and mine. In the first story, a potentially nasty conflict is avoided during a vacation; in the second, I encounter a situation that is always difficult for me

All there is to life is getting a meaning into a lot of material. You've got to come out somewhere, just as plain as a wisecrack or a joke.

—ROBERT FROST

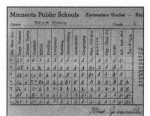

B.'s memory trigger: An elementary school report card. Remembering youthful achievements and disappointments

and see my wife in a new and endearing way.

- **Part Two. The Workbook.** This largest part of the book consists of two kinds of triggering techniques: firstly, memory maps, lists, and questions; secondly, commonplace personal experiences that both illustrate the techniques and may also trigger more memories. The personal experiences are called Story Triggers. Each triggered story is followed by a series of related questions and can trigger your memories as you read it.

Each major technique–like memory mapping–is followed by a section of Activities that can help you apply your new memories to improve relationships, creative projects, and your self-understanding in the here-and-now.

The first part of the workbook focusses on evoking childhood memories, and the techniques are adaptable to other parts of your life.

The second part turns to other parts of your life, down to the recent past. And throughout, the book emphasizes the importance of remembering yourself in the moment, which is living *consciously.* If you want to remember a dream, a sunset, or an important personal encounter before it slips away, within the process is a gentle suggestion that we become aware of the past through memories of the present experience through a heightened consciousness and mindfulness of what is happening in the moment. All our experiences–past and present–are considered to be worth remembering.

Most of the Story Triggers are mine, and others are contributed by my family and my friends. These are used, rather than memories triggered in my workshops, because of their ease of access; I have never attempted to collect memories triggered in those workshops.

- **Part Three. Epilogue.** Two personal stories that describe the use of triggering to relieve the pain of a major life trauma, and to recover memories about my father.

- **The Appendix** contains sources where you can track down other memory triggers (vintage movies, radio programs, and music), an early life questionnaire (with a parent, you reconstruct hard-to-remember memories of your early years), a reading list, acknowledgements, and information about Memory Triggering Workshops and the Proust Press.

MR. SAMMLER: I see you have these recollections.

WALLACE: Well, I need them. Everybody needs his memories. They keep the wolf of insignificance from the door.

—SAUL BELLOW
Mr. Sammler's Planet

Triggering in the Here-and-Now

(Two stories of triggering being used to enhance a couple's experiences in the here-and-now.)

Tuggin' and Pullin'

A husband's unexpected memory of himself as an unhappy little boy in a department store with his mother relieves a threat—decades later—of a very unpleasant last day of vacation with his wife.

Even the best relationships have occasional glitches and dead spots, differences in energies, rhythms, and personal preferences. Do we go to a movie or stay home, should the temperature of the house be higher or lower, does one of us need to be alone for awhile? More seriously, are any conflicts brewing just under the surface, to explode unexpectedly sometime in the future?

Those in relationships know that the crucial problems of relationship often stem from "not telling" what the problem is. So here's a story of a problem (mine) that was *not* told, and moreover could not have been. How could I

F.'s memory trigger: Listening with her family to music of holidays past (and sharing memories afterward)

tell if I was not conscious of what needed to be told? Instead, I was aware only of a deep, sullen anger toward my wife that arose in certain situations that I could not recall when I tried to be specific about them! To complicate matters, my wife, since she could not be told what I did not know, was unaware of any problem at all. Until triggering, that is.

Getting up in the morning. At home, my wife and I awake to different drummers, and we both know how to take care of ourselves. She surges out of bed around six or six-thirty, full of energy, speaks immediately and distinctly, and then quickly moves out of the house for her morning swim and then she's off to work. She has no interest in breakfast, and perhaps will swig a liquid protein drink. She's a fast-riser.

I wake up unwillingly, and it's almost *always* too early for me. I'd rather wait for the sun to appear. I move around in bed for a while, very slowly and heavily, making moaning sounds like, "oh boy, oh boy." I don't want to have a conversation or even open my eyes. In fact, I sometimes keep them closed as I sleepily answer my wife's questions about the day's plans. In an hour or so, I'll be human. But first I need to make myself a decent-sized breakfast, and have my coffee and the *Times*. It will be nine o'clock or after before I'm ready for what someone has called "peak" performance. I'm a slow-riser.

Since we leave each other early in the day, our different morning rhythms never seriously get in each others' way. *But all this changes when we're on vacation.*

It's a travel day, and we're leaving Lenox, Massachusetts to catch a plane in Boston for San Francisco, the end of a really good trip. We have plenty of time. As usual, she wants to swim and move out, perhaps by nine o'clock, and has no appetite for anything more complex than tea; I'm looking forward to a hearty New England breakfast and I could leave as late as 11 a.m. or noon. I mean, what's the hurry?

So the issue is posed, as she, already in her bathing suit, stands over me, still in bed, ready for her swim. "What time shall we leave? What about nine o'clock? I'll be finished swimming by then and my things are already in the car." Then to me, sweetly and reasonably: "We can eat on the road. When do you want to leave?"

I think, "I won't be anywhere near ready by nine o'clock. I think (but don't express this thought, since it might be construed as childish), "There's no decent food on the road back, I'll have to wait too long, and I'm hungry NOW." And then I find himself getting angry, a sharp stabbing deep anger that, even as I feel it, seems, while real, overdetermined and inappropriate.

I manage to remember that whenever I leave earlier than I want to, with the *promise* of getting something to eat soon, it never happens. It *never* happens. We can never find a restaurant on the road that pleases us both, and I get hungrier and hungrier and madder and madder. And by the time we are on the road a couple of hours I am often furious, and worse still from her point of view, grouchy.

So we don't come to an agreement and I (grumpily, even though I'm getting my way) go off alone to my lovely old-fashioned New England breakfast with French Toast and genuine maple syrup and great jam without telling her exactly when I will be back. The trouble is, seated in this lovely country inn, I am *still* angry and don't know exactly why, since I had apparently gotten exactly what I wanted. Am I having any fun yet?

A nd then suddenly a memory chooses to reappear, one I had triggered many months earlier.

The Memory *I am a very young child, being strongly*

I never intended to entertain my contemporaries with the tricks of a juggler, in the hope of being recognized as an original. I simply wanted to create around me a world of my own in which I could survive the progressive disruption going on all over the world.

—OSKAR KOKOSCHKA,
Painter

B's memory trigger: An old toy from his childhood, located in his mother's attic. (Primitive hand-fashioned sling shot and pellet, Minneota, MN, c. 1946

and uncomfortably tugged by the arm by my mother through Lord and Taylor or another New York City department store. I'm conscious of seeing mostly legs and knees, and people in motion—and I'm furious about being pulled by her agenda, furious about not being able to sit down, furious because I was tired and could not rest.

This magically appearing memory, in response to this here-and-now experience at an unhappy breakfast in Lenox, is teaching me that I was now reliving that same situation of childhood. I had felt tugged, pulled, asked to go against my needs and rhythms.

The rest is less dramatic, but very important to our relationship. My anger slowly subsided, but not entirely. I think I was now afraid that she would pay no attention to what I had discovered. At the hotel room, my wife was still *very* anxious to leave, so she asked me to tell her my big news when we were in the car. And I did, and she listened, and was interested and surprised, for she had no idea I was feeling that way. And we lived happily ever after, never having to face the problem again? Well, not quite, but that memory of Lenox remains in our consciousness, and when the issue of our differing morning rhythms needs attention, we generally remember Lenox, chuckle, and within moments—with little ado—decide when and how to get what we *both* want.

The Pleasure of My Company

With the help of a triggered memory, a very brief experience in a couple's kitchen warms their relationship and helps them to understand each other better.

Because of our divergent backgrounds and experiences my partner and I cannot expect to always agree, or to understand each other totally. But shared memories can provide new glimpses of the other's past, concerns, and inner vulnerabilities. And can often open the door to new insights about old events to enhance relationships in the here-and-now.

My partner told me, after a few years of triggering our lives: "I know you at every age." I believe that good relationships are subtly *flavored* and richly *nourished* by the sharing of the commonplace and subtle, as well as the happy and sad experiences of childhood. The following story illustrates how my wife and I used a triggering episode in the present as an unthreatening, productive, and profound way to know–really know–one another. The entire episode covered perhaps a minute or two of our lives, but it still affects my perception of my wife, and who she is, and the way I can express my love to her.

In the kitchen, Joan was preparing dinner for a family gathering, and I was in our home office, doing something or other, when I heard her asking me to join her quickly in the kitchen. I came, but she had interrupted what I had been doing, and I remembered that in the past, when she had asked me to join her, it seemed as if *nothing* special had been going on, and that she had lured me in there for nothing! I'd stand around for awhile and watch her cook, and then, because there was no place to sit down in the kitchen, my back would begin to ache, and I'd leave. So I was irritated when I arrived, expecting more of the same. And I was surprised.

Excitedly, she said: "I just had a triggering experience! I was simply stirring some turkey gravy. It was no big deal. And then I became aware of the pleasurable feelings I was having, somehow connected with the sheer *motion* of stirring the gravy. I began to wonder what had triggered those feelings, and then I had a visual memory of my grandmother in *her* kitchen. I thought of the many, many

Age does not make us childish, as they say.

It only finds us true children still.
—GOETHE

J's memory trigger: Using her grandmother's recipes

hours I spent there with her. And then when *you* walked in, I felt so loving, so safe, and so companionable!"

And a new insight arrived: "I realized that I sometimes try to lure you in here on some pretext or other because it feels so good just to have you here!"

Then another memory arose: "My kids were very small and they would be in the breakfast room and I'd be in the kitchen and there would just be lots of activity and this wonderful, warm loving ambience. And I'd feel that, 'God, the world is wonderful.' And *that's* how I felt the moment *you* walked in.

"So maybe you'll understand those kitchen feelings of mine and not be such a grouch next time!"

Out of brief, seemingly inconsequential interchanges like this one, connecting the past and present, grew enormous feelings of closeness, love and deep understanding of one another.

So every here-and-now event (leaving town on vacation, making gravy, taking a walk, reading a book, seeing a TV show, or doing a triggering exercise) has the potential of evoking a memory from the past that could be useful and life-enhancing in a journey through life together. Perhaps we will understand ourselves or the other better, or provide a story for sharing with another, for whatever it might do to enhance our relationship. Or some memories might be just for our own private selves.

Triggering has enabled us to know each other's inner lives more completely through the sharing of both joyful and painful stories of the past. It has also helped us to defuse conflict by quickly recognizing how difficult here-and-now situations can sometimes be triggered by past events, and by *defusing* them–humorously when possible–before they get out of hand.

FLYING A KITE ON A WINDY DAY

VISTING A RELATIVE OUT O

YOUR FIRST PET

THE WORKBOOK

SINGING SONGS AROUND A C

VING CROSS-COUNTRY WITH YOUR FAMILY

THE SOUND OF A FOGHORN

Triggering Guidelines

In this chapter, you will:

- Learn these and other workshop-tested requirements for successful memory triggering:

  - Capturing

  - Key Words

  - Memory Clusters

  - A Triggering Environment

  - Relaxing

We use the past to define ourselves, to deal with the present, and to prepare for the future. Memory dictates the way we express ourselves, think about ourselves, communicate with others; it is at the core of being human.

—EDITH NALLE
SCHAFER
Our Remarkable Memory

L.'s memory trigger: Going to collectibles and antique stores looking for familiar things

These are the guidelines for memory triggering I use at the beginning of my workshops. You may ignore them and still trigger memories, but I would not recommend that you take the chance. Put another way, you may be able to use this process in a noisy room, totally available for interruptions, with other things on your mind, and skipping nonchalantly from exercise to exercise, neglecting to capture what you are getting, but I suspect that you won't be satisfied with the results. As triggers usually lose their power to evoke memories with every successive use, you may not wish to accept the risk of using them casually.

Among these guidelines are those I would call absolute necessities for successful triggering, together with some available options, and some clues to mysteries you may encounter as you enter the process.

Absolute Necessities

Capture Your Memories Before They Get Away

Plan to create an immediate record of your memories. Like dreams, triggered memories are easily forgotten; once lost, we may never be able to trigger them again. By taking the simple step of capturing or recording a memory, you'll be preserving it for whatever you might want to do with it later on.

You won't know in advance which memories will prove to contain meanings of importance to improving your life. So be sure to capture whatever comes up, not only the memories you consider important at the time, but also those "far out" (why did I remember this?) memories, images and thoughts. Many months ahead, any memory may synergistically interact with another new memory, a previously stored one, or with an event going on in the here-and-now and suddenly reveal new meanings and understandings to you.

Earlier you read about a man's unhappy memories of himself as a child, being "tugged" by his mother through a department store. Suddenly–decades later–that memory connected to an unpleasant here-and-now experience of the child-become-man, feeling "tugged" in the same way by his wife, who invariably wants to leave a vacation spot and hit the road more quickly than he does. This newly acquired memory triggers memories of similar experiences in the couple's life, and results in unexpected and revealing conversation, together with the likelihood that the couple, now conscious of this "rubber band" to the past, will behave differently the next time this happens.

Using Key Words
When Capturing Your Memories

The best way to retain important memories is to quickly capture the essence of the memory with a key word or two–the name of an object, a person, an event, a feeling–that you know will re-trigger the memory later on; at any time, then, you can elaborate or expand on that memory–creating, in effect, one of the many stories of your life. When you capture key words quickly, rather than focusing on a single memory in the midst of the triggering process, you can also capture the rest of any memory cluster that may be emerging at the moment. (The neighborhood map on page 50 contains examples of several key words.)

Here's an example of a man capturing key words: He remembers himself as an early teenager, playing a game of cards with a young red-haired girl, on a ledge across the street from his apartment building on Haven Avenue in Washington Heights, Manhattan. The memory appears in the middle of a memory cluster that he also wanted to capture. So instead of staying with the single memory and perhaps losing some others, he simply writes "Vera-wall."

Memory is a shuttle. Every time you start to tell an event, you end up moving backward as well as forward.

—ARTHUR MILLER

B.'s memory trigger: Revisiting his old neighborhood. Or finding an old photo.(Washington Heights, NYC, 1940s)

Every time he sees these key words in the weeks ahead he remembers not only the details of that memory but also several related ones. So key words can re-trigger the original memory, trigger related ones, and can also be expanded or elaborated into longer stories at any time.

Where Do You Capture Your Key Words?

Sometimes, when you're creating maps, floor plans, and lists, I'll ask you to capture your key words on **8-1/2 by 11 sheets of loose-leaf paper.** At other times you have two options.

1. **The first is to use the margins in this book as a capturing device, and write directly in the wide ruled columns that you'll find on most pages.**

2. **If you prefer not to write in books, keep several small notepads handy and capture your key words in those, or on a small tape recorder. It's your choice.**

Don't be concerned if memories from different periods of your life seem to be scattered all around–in a very non-chronological order–as you're triggering. At the end of the workbook you'll learn how you can transfer all your key words to a single place and organize them in a more effective way. You may choose to arrange them chrono-logically, or group together important people, places, or key events in your life. Perhaps there's another way of organizing your key words that is more appealing to you.

You may want to begin organizing your key words before you reach the end of the workbook. If you do, you will probably trigger still more memories as you rearrange them.

You may want to create a "memory album," something like your family photograph album, but containing memories instead. Or use them to create a memoir, or contribute them to a project that would become a family legacy.

If you use a word processor, you may want to transfer your memories to computer files; if you have a desktop publishing program, you may wish to draw your memory maps on your computer (page 62). And of course you can transfer your memories to audio or video tapes at any time.

Consider carrying a notepad and perhaps your tape recorder to capture those memories that will arise spontaneously when you're away from this book. Actually, any medium for capturing is okay: the other side of a laundry receipt, a scrap of paper, whatever happens to be handy. You can always recopy these memories later to a more appropriate place.

Expect Memory Clusters

There's another reason for capturing: you may find that you are triggering more memories more quickly than you had expected, making remembering even more difficult. Your memories may arrive as part of a cluster of many, arriving almost simultaneously, and you will probably lose some with meaning and importance if you trust your now-overburdened memory to remember them all. So memories sometimes won't emerge neatly, one at a time, in a way they can be easily captured, but in "clusters."

In workshops some people report feeling temporarily overwhelmed and "flooded", and experiencing a confusing mixture of feelings and moods. If this should happen to you, just capture your key words quickly, as best you can, and return to them later. Probably the memories that come forward in a rush will be the most accessible and manageable ones (even when they are difficult), perhaps

The secret of being free is to remember.

—TRADITIONAL
GERMAN SAYING

J.'s memory trigger: Visiting her father's grave (Pittsburgh, Pa., 53 years later)

lying just under the surface of consciousness, waiting to be remembered and used.

Create the Best Possible Environment for Triggering

Under certain conditions you will remember more effectively. Your ability to remember will be affected by your surroundings and situation (horn-driven traffic or alone in the woods), by the state of your mind and your body (agitated or relaxed), and by any people you happen to be with. Most often, triggering works best in a quiet place, where your concentration will not be interrupted by telephone calls, unexpected visitors, noises, or distracting tasks. Before using these exercises, consider carefully where you could go to find that quiet space, and when, or how you can create it, so you can diminish the importance of the outside environment and focus on triggering.

I'll sometimes suggest closing your eyes to reduce any distractions in your triggering space. This can be very effective. It may not exclude sounds that appear un-expectedly: if they do, allow the sounds to simply exist in the background and see if they help you re-visit the past.

Relax Your Mind and Body

When you begin to trigger, your mind might still be in the office, or focused on a talk you just had with your partner, or on another problem of the day. This is the time to slip gently into a different and more relaxed state, something like the way you feel after you've exercised and emptied your thinking and overworked mind. Or the way you feel when falling asleep, at that midpoint between consciousness and sleep, when you sometimes receive surprising images, perhaps of a beach or countryside scene, a visitor from another generation, or a geometric pattern.

So, before you begin each exercise, I'll suggest—in the wide margins of the book—ways of relaxing that will help you to become receptive to any memories that might emerge. If you have your particular way of relaxing—perhaps playing your favorite music, doodling on a pad, or imagining being at your favorite vacation spot, do that instead. Perhaps you will want to do something physical, like exercising, before beginning. Relax your way or try one of my suggestions. Whatever you do, know that you need to be relaxed before triggering can be truly effective.

And once you identify that place of relaxation and comfort it is important in another way: if anything difficult should come up, you can call on that place—that ocean, that mountain, standing next to a friend or beloved person, a safe place known to you. Should anything emerge that makes you uneasy, or tense, or concerned that you may not be able to handle it, think about that safe place, take yourself there, stay there as long as you wish. You can always return to this material at another time, when you're more fortified.

Your Options When Triggering

You Can Go Public or Stay Private With Your Memories

You may choose to go public with some or all of your memories—most people seem to choose to share some, but the decision is yours to make. Some memories may be too personal or painful or shameful for you to ever share, even with your partner or closest friend. Some may sound like bragging, which some of us have been taught not to do.

At the other extreme, you may receive great pleasure from sharing particularly joyful experiences, significant achievements, and stories about people who were particularly

I could smell my father's pipe.

—A YOUNG MAN, *after hearing Peter, Paul, and Mary sing* Day is Done, *in 1992.*

P's memory trigger: The scent of a jar of Noxzema evoked memories of suntans and summer days at the beach with her friends

important to you (and often getting other stories back in return). Two questions: How many important people, teachers, and mentors in your life are known to even your closest friends and family? And would it be nice if they knew?

The triggering process is set up to protect you, and to respect your wishes for privacy. If someone should happen to see any of your key words, they very likely will mean little or nothing unless you choose to elaborate on them.

Choosing to Elaborate Your Key Words

At some point, perhaps very early on in the triggering process, you may choose to share some of your key words, elaborating them into stories as you do. You may do this privately while you more fully express your key words as a memoir, or journal or family legacy. And you can *share* with other people as well: one of many things you can do is to show your key words to someone and ask them to ask you questions about them. (This in turn should trigger memories of theirs.)

Actually, a key word re-visited by yourself or shared with someone else becomes an elaboration almost immediately, as the original memory becomes the core of a larger story containing subtle updating of the original memory as you add your experience and interpretation as an adult. Here's an example from a triggering workshop:

To show how elaboration and the updating of memories work, I offer to share my own neighborhood map with the group and answer questions about my key words. Someone asks, "Tell us about the three words–"Astaire-dancing home"–in the upper left-hand corner of your map (page 50)." I said something like this:

"Well, I was 11 years old or so then, and I'm leaving the old RKO Coliseum movie theater on 181st Street in

Washington Heights, in New York City. I had just seen my first Fred Astaire-Ginger Rogers movie, *Flying Down to Rio,* and I was enthralled.

> *I see this chubby little boy on the sidewalk, around 180th street on the west side of Broadway—the visual image is very precisely placed—with neighborhood stores and small buildings behind him. He's on his way home, about seven blocks away. And he's dancing, with his arms outstretched, unaware of anyone nearby! Of course it's me.*

As I'm seeing this image, I *hear* a song in my head and I know it's 'The Carioca,' from that same movie. And I'm now *feeling* the boy's joy and exhilaration, as he pretends to dance like Astaire. The entire experience fills me with delicious, pleasurable feelings, and for several moments nothing else exists in my world. And I'm just loving that little boy. He feels like not simply 'me' at a younger age, but a dear old friend I used to know. It was such a sweet experience, and I still carry that image around with me. It was a new memory as well. I don't think I had remembered that scene before."

From that point on, I begin to elaborate on that memory, sometimes intentionally, most often not. And I found that *as the original memory entered present time*, it became the core of something larger, as I begin to add myself in the here-and-now to that memory. As a full-grown and experienced adult, I begin to think about and associate to things that little boy would not have been able to consider.

With no effort on my part, that memory began to trigger others: memories associated to that same theater and time period begin to appear (the chorus girls in that same film dancing on the wings of airplanes; seeing Bing Crosby "in person" on the stage of the Coliseum at another time; chorus girls high-kicking on stage and showing just enough cleavage to excite a little boy).

Also without any planning on my part, I began to

T.'s memory trigger: Playing a childhood game with her friends or children

interpret and comment upon that memory, realizing that while I still go out of my way to see Astaire dance, and would love to be able to dance, I somehow still can't dance to anyone's satisfaction, particularly my own. I wonder what it meant in my psychological and romantic development to have a supposed upper-class hero (actually an Austerlitz from Nebraska), who wore white dinner jackets, tuxedos, and tails, and who always won the heart of a blonde, blue-eyed woman who at the beginning of their romance was totally contemptuous of him. I wonder what that first infatuation with Astaire and Rogers had to do with my life-long appreciation of music and the world of entertainment, and why I never become a performer, unless you consider teaching as performing.

Later, I will track down some of the mysteries of this memory (and others). What was the name of the film exactly? (*Flying Down to Rio*, 1933.) How old was I exactly? (11.) How many blonde unavailable women *were* in my life? (Many.) Are any other sounds, smells, or tastes, or sights associated with that memory?

Still later I would play CD's of the original music from those films and from that time period in my life, some of it my parents' music, to trigger still more memories. And so it goes. That memory of a chubby boy dancing was the beginning of a process that continues to tell me more about who I was, how I became that way, and who I am today.

Some Mysteries of Remembering

Diminishing Returns

The story of the French tea cookie, the *madeleine*, in Marcel Proust's novel *Remembrance of Things Past,* has fascinated many who have similar experiences. When the novel's hero once again smells and tastes a madeleine dipped in a cup of lime tea, as he had decades before at his aunt's house, this experience unexpectedly provides the emotional and psychological trigger for a rich recollections of his childhood. Proust believed in the power of sensory triggers. He also believed that repeated exposure to a trigger–*any* trigger–would diminish its ability to evoke memories. An example of how this works:

My first exposure to the scent of the narcissus flower was some forty years after elementary school, when I tended one on a window sill in my second grade classroom. Following this exposure, multiple images of my elementary school classroom quickly appeared in my consciousness, images of people, objects, and episodes –pleasant and not-so-pleasant–that happened there. A few months later, I smelled another narcissus flower but the experience was different. My feelings were less strong and sweet, and I had memory or two, but these were mostly elaborations of the ones I had already triggered. Still later, I smelled a narcissus flower once more. I was able to simply enjoy the scent, which was now detached from any memories at all.

For this reason I'd discourage anyone from sampling the exercises without honoring the guidelines, perhaps hoping to see what the experience is like and whether they really want to go further. If you should do this, you should know that a powerful trigger may not work during its second–and more serious–application. The trigger's power may be reduced or diminished altogether, and you may lose the opportunity to recall and use the memories it would evoke.

The most important things in life cannot be measured or quantified.

–JACK GIBB,
Philosopher

B.'s memory trigger: The smell and feel of a bear from childhood. Recovered by his Mom from the family attic.

Prepare to Deal with the Unexpected

Before beginning to trigger, people ask me questions about the process. How many memories can I expect to get? Will there be many or few? Will they be pleasant or painful? Will they be accurate? How will I know? Can I believe what I remember?

How many? In my workshops, some people get hundreds of memories, others dozens, and some only a few. Some get exactly what they wanted and others get something less or more. Some get most of their memories during the first days of triggering. Later they may trigger others, elaborate on the ones they have already triggered, share them with others, and find important life-meanings revealed to them. All of this can happen spontaneously, without any help from the triggering techniques.

How pleasant or painful? Triggering techniques do not encourage remembering the dark side of life, but instead assist you to remember only what you choose to remember. Since everyone's life is a mixture of pleasure and pain, you will probably trigger both pleasurable and painful events from your life. The proportion of one to the other will depend on your life experience, your tolerance for inner exploration, and your willingness to remember. You may, as I have done, remember mostly pleasant or bittersweet experiences and recall truly painful episodes only rarely.

When you invite your memories into your present life, you can expect your feelings about them to change. You won't remember an event with the same feelings you had while it was happening (a girl being shoved by an older boy on her way to school, another girl terrified of going down the basement stairs). Instead, you'll remember such experiences as an *observer:* the older person you are today—a person with perspective, skills, and life-experiences not possessed by any child. Except in rare cases, these past events are not *re-experiences* but simply memories that you can now use in a positive way: to improve a relationship, learn more about yourself, or create an important project.

And if a memory is too painful? Immediately shift your mind to a particularly pleasant place in your life (perhaps a favorite home, or a grandmother's house) and return to triggering only when you are ready. Later, you may wish to seek assistance from a close friend, counselor, or spiritual guide. And particularly from a partner or loved one; your experience together can then be richer, more exciting, and more rewarding.

How accurate can you expect your memories to be? For most people, this will be an unanswerable question, because it's so difficult to judge or referee the precise details of our memories. Perhaps a memory—the first time it is remembered—is what we might call accurate—although it may actually be a memory of a childhood fantasy, a dream, or a story told to you by someone else. Whether it "happened" or not, a memory is surely **updated** every time it is remembered, with new material added from our more recent knowledge and experience. You will see examples of this updating in the triggered memories presented in this book.

This seems to matter more than accuracy as you trigger your memories: First, since you had a reason for triggering that memory from the countless number that were available for you to draw from, you can assume that the memory is somehow important. Second, it is in your best interest to remember the details as accurately as you can, while recognizing that it is the *meaning and understanding* that memories can provide, as well as the here-and-now uses you can put it to, that really matter, whether you can ever settle the question of accuracy or not.

None of us will get through life without some pie in our face. Whether our life is comic or tragic may ... depend upon our tolerance for the inevitable indignities. Would it really be so awful if, in surviving, we dribbled a little food on our tie?

—FRANK PITTMAN, M.D.

B's memory trigger: Re-reading a favorite book from childhood

Some words of advice: If you are in personal therapy, or belong to a therapeutic group of any kind, show this book to your counselor before you begin to do the exercises. The exercises are not intended to replace any personal therapy or therapy group you might be involved in or belong to, but they might enhance the work you are doing. Your counselor would be in the best position to advise you how to go ahead and perhaps incorporate these exercises into your therapeutic work.

So—expect nothing, and be ready for anything: a good creed to follow when triggering, since memory triggering, like living, is more magical than scientific, often thrilling and sometimes a little frightening. As this process has been developed, I have seen the magic work in my own life and on the lives of many others. I hope that your memories will be helpful in illuminating the meaning and importance of your life, at enriching your creative life and your relationships, and help you come to a sense of peace with your life and your accomplishments.

Now—on to memory triggering! I hope you get what you want!

Mapping Your Childhood Neighborhood

In this chapter, you will:

- Learn seven important tips for effectively using the mapping technique

- Recreate a neighborhood of your childhood, triggering memories along the way

- Learn three ways to use your memories creatively, for self understanding, and in relationships

- Discover whether another's memory of "first love" questions trigger similar memories of yours

These are these woods we weren't supposed to go through! But it was a shortcut to school, and everybody said how dangerous it was, so of course I did it. It felt like just the naughtiest thing you could do, because some "bad people" hung out in there. Probably big boys and men—God knows who they all were, but there was this funny feeling about it. And of course it was a marvelous place to play, great big trees, and we'd have our own path.

When we'd be late to school, we'd take another way. And I always hoped that the Josephs wouldn't be looking out their window and catch us going in a direction we weren't supposed to go in. He was so stern and my step-father's friend. I think I must have gotten caught once going through there.

—JOAN, 61

On the following pages: The author's neighborhood map. Washington Heights, New York City, 1928-1934.

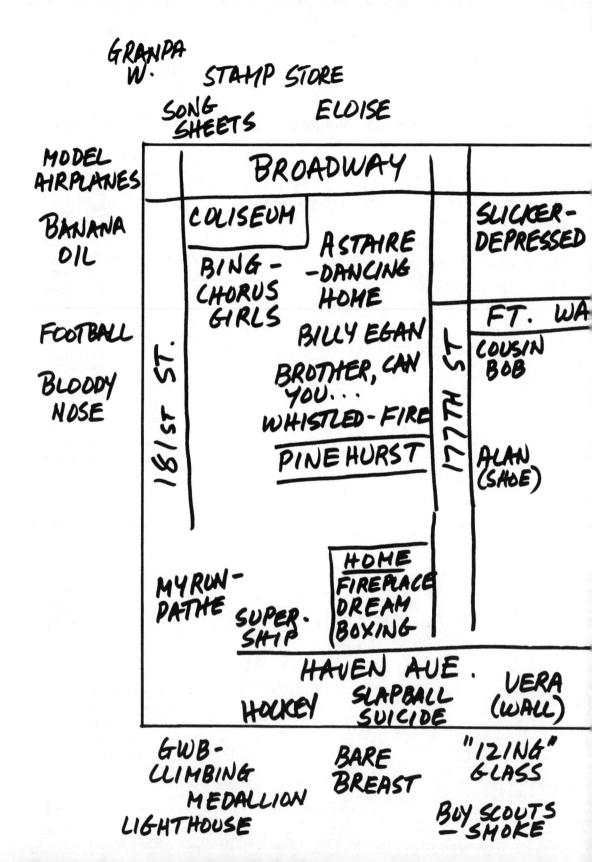

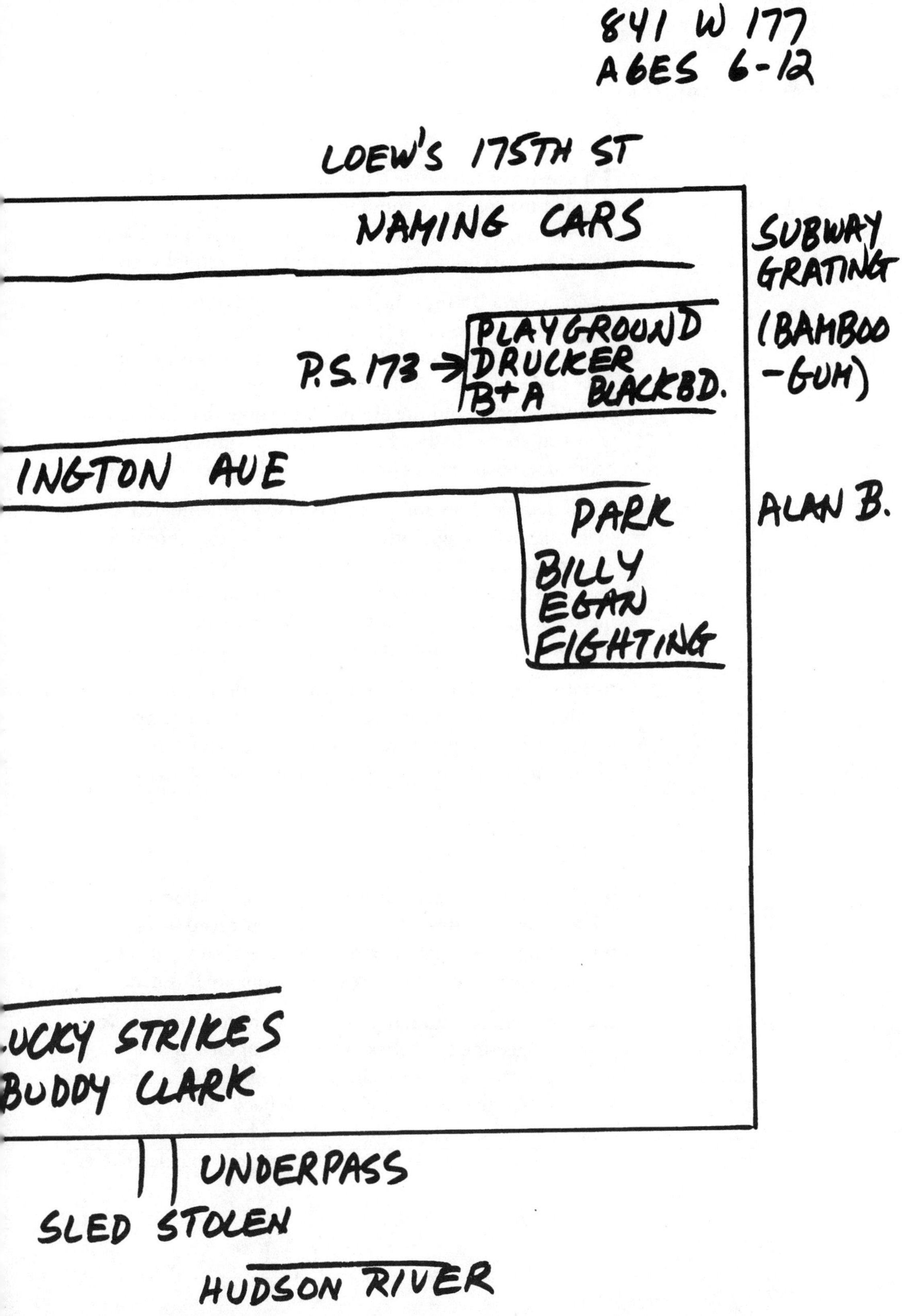

LOEW'S 175TH ST

NAMING CARS

SUBWAY
GRATING

P.S. 173 → PLAYGROUND
DRUCKER
B+A   BLACKBD.

(BAMBOO
–GUM)

INGTON AVE

PARK
BILLY
EGAN
FIGHTING

ALAN B.

UCKY STRIKES
BUDDY CLARK

UNDERPASS

SLED STOLEN

HUDSON RIVER

In this first exercise we'll use the triggering technique called mapping. As you draw this map, you'll begin to trigger and collect memories of important people, places, events, and feelings from your elementary school years.

As you reflect on these memories, and on others you will trigger during the other exercises, they may remind you of what was meaningful and formative during this period of your life, and also reveal something about your strengths, your sore spots, and the events and people that influenced who you are today. Further on in the workbook, you'll begin to add memories of other periods of your life.

You'll discover how some of your newly remembered memories will trigger others and how you can choose to elaborate some "key words" into longer stories—for your own self-understanding, for creative projects like journals, memoirs, and family histories, and for enhancing your relationships with important people in your life.

As you trigger, I'll also remind you to capture your key words as you go, and to organize them, at least temporarily, as a first step toward building a permanent and useful supply of your childhood memories.

The Icons

Whenever you see this hand 🖐, stop reading and follow the instructions you have just read before proceeding. Immediately capture any memories you are getting. Then return to the text when you are finished.

Even now, before beginning to actually create your map, you may be triggering memories in the form of images or thoughts or feelings. If you are, be sure to capture them–as key words–in the wide margins of this book, or, if you'd rather not write in the book, in a notepad you can always carry with you. You can transfer them to your map later. 🖐

Making Ready

Tape together two sheets of your supply of 8-1/2 by 11 paper to make one large sheet. Choose whatever writing or drawing materials, of whatever color, you like the best. And as always have your supplies handy.

You may also want to re-read the guidelines for triggering on page 35 before beginning each exercise, until you're totally familiar with the concepts of capturing, key words, and relaxing before triggering.

Prepare your supplies and re-read the guidelines if you wish. Then return to the text. ✋

Seven Tips

1. Because this is the first time you'll be using mapping, you may find that large clusters of memories are coming into your consciousness all at once, perhaps more than you think you can handle. You may feel flooded and somewhat frightened. If this should happen, capture key words for as many memories as you can. Avoid any memories you don't wish to deal with at the moment. If your map seems too small to contain all the memories you're triggering, use your wide margins (or your notepad).

2. Use the wide margins also for capturing key words of any memories you trigger from other time periods that don't belong on this particular map. Later, you can transfer these key words to the appropriate time period.

3. If you lived in more than one home, and went to more than one school, map one of these trips only. Decide now which home and which school you will map, and then return to the text.

4. Don't worry about these things: gaps in your

Old age is very democratic. With the wisdom of hindsight we can see that any life, if described in emotional terms, is just as important as any other.

–ROBERT PLUNKET,
novelist

G.'s memory trigger: A compact disk of theme songs from TV shows of the 70s and 80s

If you wish, you can use these wide margins for capturing your key words.

memory (expect some), the number of memories you are getting (there's no correct number), drawing your map to exact scale (not what triggering is about), or becoming confused between one place or time and another (just do the best you can for now; you may be able to correct the confusion later.)

5. Regard everything you remember as valuable and worthy of being remembered, no matter how trivial it may seem at the moment. Try not to judge the significance of your memories. Capture them first and consider their importance later.

6. Before beginning, be certain that your physical space has been liberated from possible distractions —interruptions by other people, telephone calls, street or other noises, and so on. Give yourself at least two hours for this exercise, preferably longer. You may need less time, but don't count on it: once in a triggering mood, you may not want to interrupt your mood and your flow of memories and thoughts.

7. And be sure to quiet your mind and body, so your memories can rise easily into consciousness, unobstructed by daily pressures and concerns. For triggering to work, you need to take command of your personal energy, removing any obstacles to focussing on what is ahead. One simple but powerful way to do this (there are many, and some will be described in the book) is to get in touch with your breathing patterns. Try this now, and perhaps every time you begin a new exercise: Deeply breathe in, through the nose, hold it, then let it out slowly, through the mouth. Do this several times, until you become more deeply relaxed and feel more energy becoming available to be focused on what you are about to do.

As I mentioned earlier, you can also use my suggestions for relaxation exercises in the wide margins of these exercises. **Now relax in any way you choose, and return to the text with your mind and body relaxed and free of any distractions.** 👋

Recreating Your Neighborhood

In the upper-right-hand corner of your mapping paper, write or print the following: your name, your ages during the time you lived in the home and school you have chosen to map (for example, 7-13); the years covered by this time period (say, 1950-1956); your home address at the time, and the name of your school. (Don't be concerned if you don't remember all of this information. Write down what you can and research the rest when you can.) Be as complete as you can and capture any memories you are getting as you do this simple task. Begin now and when you're done, return to the text. 👋

First you need to recreate the "neighborhood" of your childhood. This is an area contained by boundaries not pictured on your ordinary map: the area most familiar to you during your childhood years, where you were probably allowed to roam by yourself, where you spent the most time, and where you may have felt most safe when you were alone. Your neighborhood may have been large or small, and its boundaries were probably defined by your parents or other elders. Your school may be located within this neighborhood, but perhaps not.

So you will visit not only your neighborhood, but also the area directly "outside" your neighborhood, for memories of places, people, and events that perhaps felt less safe, or more exciting, than your usual haunts.

The completed neighborhood map on page 50 shows a wide margin separating memories of my urban

Before beginning the exercise, say these words slowly to yourself:

"I will do the mapping exercise any way I like. It can be simple or complex, artistic or very rough. I can draw it as an adult would, or in the style of the child I was in those years.

"As I draw my map, I'll try to see myself on the streets of my neighborhood ...going from my house to my school...and noticing all the streets in-between ...and what happened on those streets.

"I'll try to be in touch with my feelings during those walks or drives to school –five days a week except for holidays and illnesses for all those years. What *was* I thinking and feeling during those times?

"When I draw those streets, I'll press down *hard* on the paper with my pencil or pen...as if I were walking with my own weight there...and try to *feel* myself on those streets again so I can remember what happened there!"

Return to the text when you're ready.

"neighborhood"–the larger "inside" area–from memories of "outside" my neighborhood (within the smaller "border.") Study the map now. If you are getting any memories, be sure to capture them as they arise; then return to the text. ✋

1. *Welcome back.* Now begin to think about the shape and boundaries of your neighborhood. (Was it horizontal, rectangular, or oddly shaped at some places?) With your eye focused on your mapping paper and perhaps intermittently closing your eyes, imagine yourself as a bird, high above your neighborhood, looking down. Imagine the location of your home within the neighborhood boundaries. How far could you, did you, go in each direction? Those outer limits will become the outline of your neighborhood. ✋

2. On your mapping paper, mark each of the four boundaries of your neighborhood, one by one, and draw your outline of your neighborhood. Leave blank the area, perhaps two inches wide, on all four sides of your paper; this smaller area will contain any out-of-neighborhood memories that you trigger. Take all the time you need, capturing any memories you get, at whatever place on your map they were triggered. ✋

3. Now focus your attention on the borders of your map–the outer limits of your neighborhood. Ask yourself: What happened just barely inside the neighborhood? What happened outside the neighborhood? Capture–as key words–any memories of this border territory. Take as much time as you need, returning to the text only when you are absolutely ready. ✋

5. *Welcome back.* Now position your home and your school on the map, in their approximate relationship to one another. (If your school was not in your

neighborhood, place it in the margin of your map.) Draw each building as a simple square or rectangle. You can do more elaborate drawings of your home and school later on, in other exercises. As you do this, capture any other memories that emerge. ✋

6. Now place your writing instrument at the place on your map where you have placed your home, and imagine yourself as a child, leaving your home to walk or be driven to school. Beginning at your door, and imagining yourself as the child you were, map the way you went to school, capturing any memories you get. Press your writing instrument firmly on the paper. Map the streets or roads you travelled, and also nearby streets or roads that you were familiar with, naming them if you can. As you map, you will remember people, places, events, and feelings that happened on those streets or in adjoining buildings. As you remember, immediately write a key word or phrase to remind you of that memory later on, at the exact place on the map where the memory occurred. Do this now, and take your time. ✋

7. *Welcome back.* Slowly review your map and the memories you have triggered, pausing at each key word and adding to your map any memories of the scents, sounds, and other sensory impressions of your neighborhood. Ask yourself: Was there, related to this neighborhood memory, something else that you smelled? (the scent of a flower or football?); heard? (the sound of a railroad train or someone's music?); tasted? (the taste of a special treat?); felt? (the feel of jacks, a barbie doll, or a favorite toy?); or saw? Do this now, and ask these questions of all the memories you trigger from now on. ✋

Welcome back. I hope you enjoyed and were fascinated by your trip to your past. You may wish to continue or stop for now. If you decide to stop now, you can return to your childhood map over and over again, possibly to evoke more memories, possibly also to trigger insights and meanings about who you were in those days, and how that small person has grown and still lives inside of you today. At the end of each triggering exercise, you'll find several things you can do to use these memories, and perhaps trigger still more memories–when you're alone and also with others.

Using Your Memories in the Here-and-Now

Activities for you to do, and to do with friends and family

1. To enhance an important relationship, consider showing your childhood map to someone close to you. Encourage that person to ask you questions about what they see so you can elaborate on your key words and phrases. Share as much or as little of each memory as you wish. Sometimes your map or memories may stimulate the memories of others. Then you can talk about similar or different experiences in both your lives. Ask questions about what they remember.

2. Choose any key word that attracts you at the moment, think about that key word, and begin to write about that person or incident for ten minutes without stopping. Write whatever comes to mind, no matter how strange it may seem. Don't judge or censor your thoughts or your writing. When you're finished, cross out (or cut away with scissors) anything you don't care for. Save what is left in a notebook or file folder or transfer what you like to a computer file.

3. If you have a tape recorder, choose any key words
    that attract you and begin to talk about them into
    the recorder, for as long as you like. Don't rewind.
    Label the tape, "Childhood Memories." Return to it
    the next time you want to elaborate on a memory
    you have captured. (Save the recording for your
    grandchildren–they'll be fascinated!)

The Story Triggers

If you're like me, you have found that you're often
triggered into remembering (and sharing) stories of your
own experiences by the personal stories that your friends
tell you, and the stories that you find in newspapers,
novels, films, or on TV. The following triggered memory,
together with the questions at the end of the memory, may
help you trigger some memories of your own. You'll find
several other Story Triggers throughout the book.

**(Continue to capture whatever thoughts, images,
feelings or sensory impressions are evoked for you.)**

First Love

I'm in the first or second grade of elementary school,
walking with my parents on the edges of my
neighborhood in Washington Heights, probably coming
home from a Chinese restaurant, and on a street where I
would feel unsafe if I were by myself. As I re-remember the
scene not long afterwards, it reminds me of a French
Impressionist painting of a couple with umbrella on a
rainy street in 19th Century Paris. (As a child, I went with
our class to see the Egyptian mummies at the
Metropolitan Museum of Art—could I have seen the
painting then?)

My parents are in the left foreground, I'm in the center
foreground. On the far corner, upper left, I see this little

About this memory:
This memory, triggered
by my neighborhood
map, appeared with
a complex mix of
emotions: childish
excitement, sadness,
regret, feeling like a
man and a boy at the
same moment... And a
wonderful sense of
being alive and real! As I
developed the triggering
method, I came to
believe that memories
▼p. 60

with **feeling** were the ones I sought.

I learned also that a seemingly unimportant childhood memory would reveal its *meaning* not at the moment of triggering but later, when it began to spontaneously become connected to other memories and with experiences I was having at the moment. It would then become *updated*, without any effort on my part, to reveal new and important insights.

As I triggered more memories about that little boy I used to be, I felt newly tender feelings toward him. And I was sad for him too, aware of the pain he would experience during his life. From that point on, I loved that little boy in a different, more connected, way.

girl from my class. She's with her parents, quite far away. She's blonde and very pretty. I'm not sure about her name and I don't know now if I ever talked with her, but I've always thought of her as Eloise, because a girl of that name, many years later, reminded me of her.

I'm very excited, pointing to her and telling my folks, "She's from my class!" Maybe I yelled to the little girl, but probably not, because that would have made too much of a fuss and my mother wouldn't have liked it. And that's the memory.

At some point, "Eloise" became the leading figure of my pre-sleep fantasies, and of recurring dreams as well. As a heroic fireman, I would rescue her from a second-story window. Then (probably as a reward for the rescue), I would get to perform, having now become a Park Avenue surgeon, some sort of (perfectly safe) operation on her beautiful (nude, unyielding) body. My influences? Besides hormones, you mean? Perhaps Pearl White bound to the railroad tracks in those cliffhanger Saturday morning movie serials I used to see, with a little Dracula thrown in?

Through the years I have met many Eloises–first Ginger, then Doris, Juliet, Eloise, Jean, Ann, Lisa, Val, Annie, Kathy, at least three others whose names have slipped my mind, and finally Margaret–mostly blonde, beautiful, and all as unattainable as Dante's Beatrice. But that's another story.

What Do *You* Remember?

Capture any memories you get as you answer these questions. Consider sharing your answers and memories with friends and family, and asking them about similar experiences in their lives. Reflect carefully on each question before moving on.

1. Do you remember anything about your first love? His or her name, family, where he or she lived, the times

you spent, what you did? Did your parents or other family members know about your first love? If they did, how did they react? How did you react?

As you read these questions, stop after each one and give yourself plenty of time to remember. Don't rush. Notice what's going on in your mind and your body. ✋

2. Do your remember your first kiss? When it happened, where, and with whom?

    Imagine sharing some of your answers with a partner or friend. Perhaps you'd want to ask them some of these same questions. ✋

3. Make a list, beginning with your first love, of all the "loves" in your life. (Perhaps you will add now-forgotten names and trigger more memories; capture them.) Alongside each name, write whatever specifics you can remember: Physical characteristics. Where they came from or went to. How you spent time with him or her. What particular episodes you remember. What happened to them? The last time you saw them? What happened then? ✋

4. When you're finished, study your list and see if you can identify any ways they are alike. And ways that they were different. Have your memories revealed anything new or interesting about the men and women in your life? ✋

On the following pages: Bob Borson, a professional writer, used his computer to recreate the farmyard of his childhood in Minneota, MN. He drew his map with a MacIntosh, MacDraw, and Microsoft Word. He first drew his map, inserting numbers at each location in the farmyard where he triggered a memory, and then quickly wrote key words about that memory before returning to the map. Later, he elaborated some of these memories into full-fledged stories.

FARMYARD

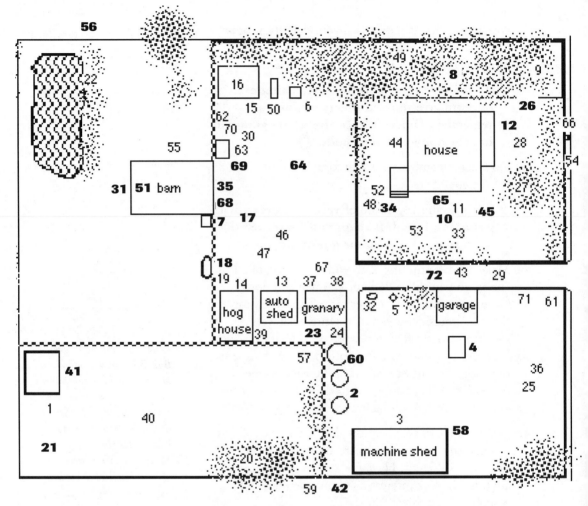

Selected Key Words from Farmyard Map

2) Rats under cribs. Scotty, the rat terrier.

4) Baby chicks in brooder house. Peat bedding. Painting pecked chickens with tar.

7) Grinding corn for cows on Saturdays. Dust and noise. Least favorite job.

8) Playing store in grove with Bonnie, using old cans and bottles.

10) Standing on head on lawn, gripping grass for balance. Smell of grass and evening air. Unquenchable thirst.

12) Playing hopskotch with Bonnie on sidewalk.

17) Pulling rope with tractor to hoist bundles of loose alfalfa into hay mow. Sweet smell of hay.

18) Drinking water from speckled blue enamel cup at tank after coming in from field on hot day.

21) Running from bull as young child (even though he wasn't chasing me).

23) Shooting sparrow—first kill with my new BB gun. Mixture of achievement and sadness. "Look what I done, Mom."

26) Picking and eating chokecherries. How they made mouth pucker.

31) Painting barn from skimsy scaffold. Seeing Dad almost fall.

34) Rolling down sidewalk in makeshift cart I put together. Wanting to be an inventor when I grew up.

35) Trying to climb rope to peak of barn hand-over-hand.

41) Falling from animal loading ramp and getting bloody nose.

42) Getting shot in the side with .22 rifle.

45) Playing catch with Dad in front yard with baseball.

51) Jumping off platform in haymow into soft hay.

56) Taking cows to pasture down lane. Developing special way of swinging arms to ward off mosquitoes.

58) Eating juicy plums from tree by machine shed.

60) Slipping off trailer and gouging left leg on metal attached to tin shed.

64) Scattering chicken feed in shapes of letters, animals, etc.

65) Getting stung by wasp while putting up screens.

68) Culling chickens. Imagining lice crawling all over me.

69) Raising deer mice in milkhouse.

72) Seeing Skeeters get run over by tractor.

Your Elementary School

In this chapter, you will:

- Draw a floor plan of your neighborhood school, triggering memories as you do

- Learn more ways to use your memories creatively, for self-understanding, and in relationships

- Read another's memories of school that may trigger more memories of yours

It was the darndest thing. I was in my late 20s, back on a visit to my old neighborhood, and I decided to revisit my elementary school, and my favorite teacher from 6th grade, Miss Farmer. She was still there, and the first thing I asked her was: When had the school been remodelled? The rooms, the halls, the stairwells, all seemed smaller. She laughed. 'No, it hasn't been remodelled, but everyone asks the same thing! You think it's smaller because your body takes up more space now!'

– BOB, 64

On the following pages: Ann's remembered floor plans of her parochial school, with key words included. Madison, Wisconsin, 1965.

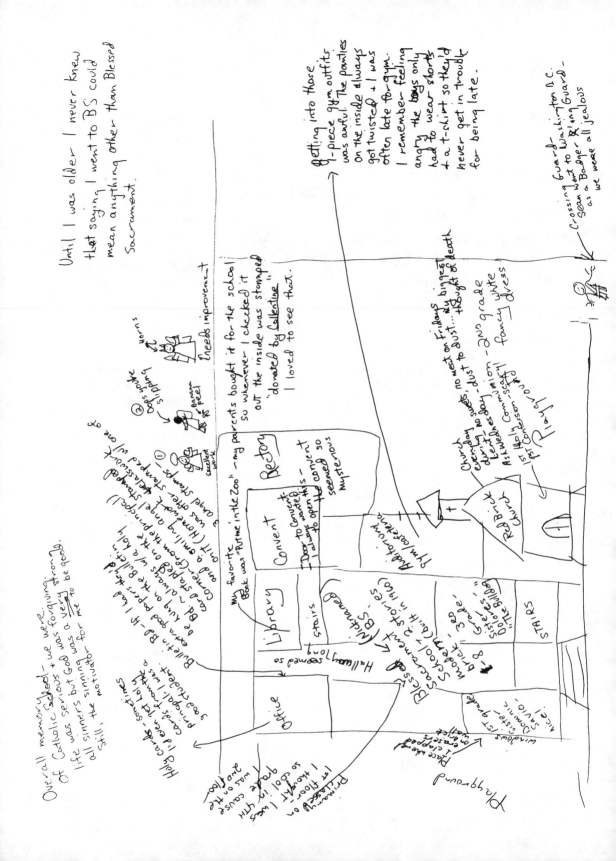

Until I was older I never knew that saying I went to BS could mean anything other than Blessed Sacrament.

Getting into those 1-piece gym outfits was awful. The panties on the inside always got twisted + I was often late for gym. I remember feeling angry the boys only had to wear shorts + a t-shirt so they'd never get in trouble for being late.

Crossing Guard - Sean went to Washington D.C. as Crossing Guard - got a Badge - we were all jealous

Overall memory of Catholic School + we were very forgiving/strong. Life was serious but God was a ___ to be good. All sinners sinning for me to ___. Still, the motivator for me to ___.

Needs improvement

horns
@ Bob's house
St. John's
Banana Feet

excellent work

Office

Library

Convent

Rectory

Stairs

Hallway seemed so long

My favorite Book was "Put me in the Zoo" — my parents bought it for the school so whenever I checked it out the inside was stamped "donated by Valentine". I loved to see that.

Door to Convent - I always wanted to open this - the convent seemed so mysterious

Auditorium w/ gym

Blessing ___ School (Middle BS)

Church every day - no sweets - dust to dust... my biggest thought of death
Lent/Ash Wednesday - 2nd grade
Ask Wednesday Communion - 2nd grade
1st Holy Communion - scary!
1st Confession - ??
Prayer

8 - 3rd grade "brick building" (convent in 1940) Sisters' Dojo Bulldog

Red Brick Church

STAIRS

windows
1st grade - Dominic Sister Savior Nice!

Playground

Place where I slapped + clapped the erasers

Primarily on 1st floor or 4th floor - I was always in the loop so...

Holly cards - sometimes 2 principal + was ___ parents as 6 Bulletin Bd - 4th ___

Playground

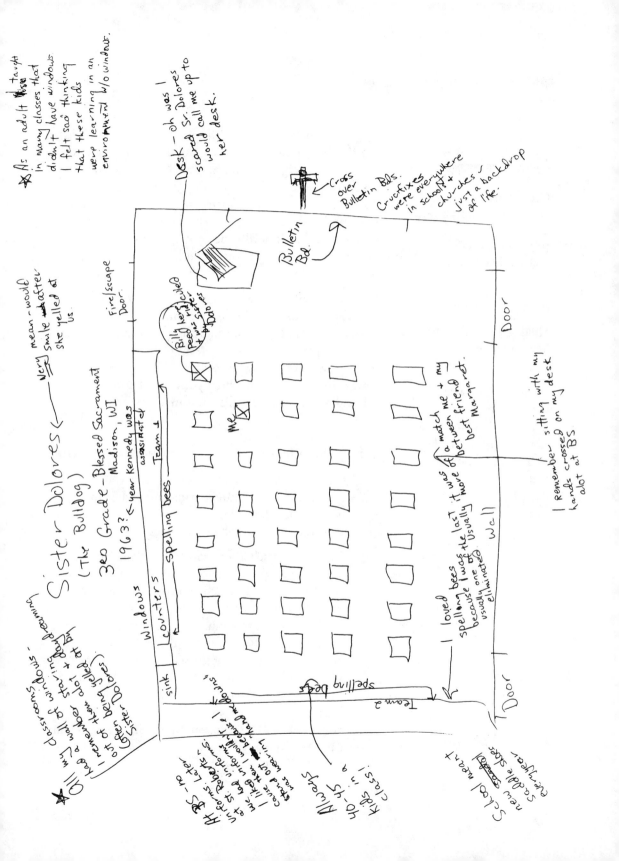

As an adult those taught in many classes that didn't have windows I felt sad thinking that these kids were learning in an environment w/o windows.

Desk — oh was I scared Sr. Dolores would call me up to her desk.

Cross over Bulletin Bds.

Crucifixes were everywhere in school + churches — just a backdrop of life.

Bulletin Bd.

Fire/escape Door

Billy kept pulling Peg's hair til I was Sister Dolores

Sister Dolores ←
(The Bulldog)
3rd Grade — Blessed Sacrament
Madison, WI
1963? ← year Kennedy was assassinated

Very mean — would smile + after she yelled at us.

My wall of staring windows — I remember them yelled at a lot of being yelled (often Sister Dolores)

Windows | Counters | sink

Team 1 — spelling bees

Me

I loved spelling bees because I was the last it was a match between me + my best friend Margaret. Usually move Usually one of eliminated

Wall

I remember sitting with my hands crossed on my desk alot at BS

Door

Door

Team 2 — spelling bees

A simple and effective way to relax before beginning to trigger:

Get in touch with your breathing patterns now, and perhaps every time you begin a new exercise, like this:

Deeply breathe in through your nose.

Hold your breath, then let it out slowly, through your mouth.

Do this several times, until you become more deeply relaxed and feel more energy available to be focused on what you are about to do. ✋

Welcome back. In the first exercise, you have revisited your childhood neighborhood. You may wish to look at your neighborhood map again, perhaps to trigger more memories, before beginning this second exercise. This time, I'll ask you to focus on a single place in your neighborhood–your elementary school–and to draw, as well as you can (it needn't be complete or perfectly drawn), a floor plan of your school, seeking more memories as you do.

Once again, liberate your triggering space from possible interruptions that would distract your flow of memories. Quiet your mind and your body as well by again getting in touch with your breathing patterns or by using your favorite way of relaxing yourself. **Take your time, and return to the text only when your mind and body are relaxed and free of any distractions.** ✋

Triggering Memories of Elementary School

Welcome back. For a few minutes, before you actually begin to draw, read these paragraphs while imagining the way you school looked when you were a child. Capture any memories you are getting in the margins. ✋

1. Imagine yourself at the entrance to your school, at the beginning of a school day. By "entrance" I mean the doors through which you passed, wherever they were. Imagine yourself standing outside at the entrance, about to go in. Are you in front of the entrance now? Is anyone else there? Are you conscious of the rest of the school building or other structures around you? What season of the year is it as you imagine the building? What is the weather like? Is it raining? Snowing? Sunny? Warm? Cold? Are you aware of any scent you can smell or sounds you can hear? Did anything important ever happen just outside that building, or nearby? ✋

2. Now imagine yourself going inside the door. Can you imagine any change of scent or odor as you step inside? Do you hear anything? To get to your classroom or wherever your class assembled, did you need to climb steps and hold on to a bannister? Or did you stay on the same floor? Now, if you can, find your way to your classroom. Does your classroom have a special odor or sounds? ✋

3. *Welcome back.* On a sheet of your triggering paper, draw a plan of the school floor you remember best, including such rooms as you remember: the classroom, the bathroom, principal's office, the auditorium, the schoolyard... If your school had more than one floor, create additional floor plans for the other floors if you wish. All the floors may fit on a single sheet, but you can use additional sheets if you like. Don't be concerned if you don't exactly remember every dimension of every space. Just draw what you remember and leave the rest blank. ✋

4. *Welcome back.* Now transfer any key words of school memories you have written earlier in the margins, in your notepad, or your neighborhood map to your floor plan, capturing any new memories that may be triggered as you do this. ✋

5. Now look over the memories you have captured on your new floor plan. Review it slowly, pausing at each key word, and asking:

Was there, related to this school memory, something else that you...

- **Smelled?** (the scent of a lunchbox?)

- **Heard?** (the sound of assembly music?)

- **Tasted?** (the taste of a certain food?)

- **Felt?** (the feel of an eraser, blackboard, or... ?)

If you wish, you can use these wide margins for capturing your key words.

• **Saw?** (something else that happened in your schoolroom?) ✋

Ask these questions of all your new memories from now on. Add any new memories that are triggered. Store your school plan together with your neighborhood map in a safe place. You will use them again.

Using Your Memories in the Here-and-Now

Activities for you to do, and to do with friends and family

1. Consider showing your floor plan to someone close to you, encouraging that person to ask you questions about the meaning of your key words and phrases. Perhaps your map or memories will stimulate someone else's. If it does, ask questions about what they remember.

2. Ask your parents or old neighborhood friends what they remember about your neighborhood school.

3. If you can, re-visit your old school. Bring a camera and your notebook. Ask for a favorite teacher. See if you can visit a classroom or the playground during recess, and be aware of what you are thinking and remembering. Study the children's faces. How is the school different than you remembered it?

To Fight or Not to Fight

About these memories:
The first was triggered by my neighborhood map; the second when drawing a floor plan of my childhood home. This was not the first time I had remembered either incident. ▶ p. 71

The school had a playground attached, and a park with a ball field just across the street, but I rarely went to either place, perhaps because they were right at the edge of my neighborhood, and I don't remember knowing anyone who stayed in that area after school. Maybe those who did lived nearby. I preferred to play on a block adjoining our apartment building. But I did play on the ball field once, and that's when I met Billy Egan, during a pickup game.

Running out a single, I accidentally squashed his foot as I crossed first base. I never knew which one of us had been clumsy, but there was no older person to moderate, and I did not ask for support. First came his challenge to fight, which I refused, and then his vow to "get" me. I was stunned, didn't know what to do.

My problem was, I had to walk by his ground-floor apartment window on my way to the stores or to run errands for my mother, and he always seemed to be there, challenging me. I never accepted. I often walked down another street, ashamed, when I suspected he would be at the window.

I was confused by this entire situation because he was the son of our school janitor, whom I liked and admired. I thought, perhaps he could do something about this. But I didn't go to him, or my father. I simply had no idea of what to do.

■ ■ ■

When I was eight or nine, a young neighbor received a pair of boxing gloves as a gift, and announced that a tournament would be held in his apartment down the hall. An older boy, perhaps a brother, would be the referee. Some space was cleared and a small rug in the boy's bedroom became the ring.

By then, my peaceful disposition was probably well-known in the neighborhood (I never got into fights), so I was matched with a boy much smaller than I. Surprising myself, I promptly decided to bash the hell out of him, and realized I was enjoying myself tremendously. After I landed five or six strong blows to the now-screaming boy's head, I also ignored the referee's call to retreat to a neutral corner of the rug. Angrily he pulled me off, unlaced my gloves, and sent me down the hall in disgrace.

Now these memories—the source of much of my childhood fear, shame, and confusion—were experienced in a larger context of other captured memories that could provide new insights and understandings. As a child, I never understood how they related to one another; like most children, I dealt with my experience incident by incident, feeling them but unable to make much sense of them.

Having *captured* them, I could connect and experience them *together*, within the broader context of my life. In this instance, I was able to truly understand a major issue and theme of my developing life: should I, or should I not, fight for what I wanted?

Of course it wasn't funny at all, despite the way I tell it. I carried my shame to my bed for many months, dreamed about my disgrace, and never shared my feelings with anyone. Looking back, I can understand that my confusion about my strength, whatever it was, and my parents' messages about aggression–what was appropriate and what was not–intensified with each new confrontation.

What Do *You* Remember?

Capture any memories you get as you answer these questions. Consider sharing your answers and your memories with friends and family, and asking them about similar experiences in their lives. Reflect carefully on each question before moving on.

1. Have any fights–fights you were in, or saw, as a child, either physical or verbal–stuck in your memory? ✋

2. What you were taught about fighting as a child? Did you get the same messages from your mother and your father? If you have brothers and sisters, how did your parents respond when you fought with them? ✋

3. How did you protect yourself–physically or verbally–from older children, children your own age, and bullies? Do you "fight" the same way now as you did when a child? ✋

Your Classroom

In this chapter, you will:

- Draw a floor plan of your school classroom, triggering memories as you do

- Learn more ways to use your memories creatively, for self-understanding and in relationships

- Discover whether another's classroom memories trigger more of yours

The other day, I was at a legal seminar, and I remembered something, but I think my body remembered before my mind did? The lecturer was illustrating something on the blackboard and at some point it was all covered with chalk and writing. And I simply had to leave my seat and do something about it! So I did, while he had stopped talking for a minute! And it felt so good! The teacher was really annoyed. He said, 'Why are you erasing the board? You're not eight years old anymore!' I knew that, but my body felt so great doing it. Some people just don't understand such things!

–MARTA, 29

Before you begin this exercise, relax yourself the way you normally do, or try deep breathing (page 68), or try this:

With your eyes closed, imagine yourself as a child, eating your favorite piece of candy.

Do you remember its name? Do you remember how you unwrapped it?

Can you imagine how it tasted, how it smelled, how it felt to the touch?

Let yourself freely associate to whatever thoughts, images, and feelings you are having.

Now close your eyes, opening them to begin the exercise when you are ready.

Welcome back. In this exercise, we'll stay in school awhile longer, as you will be drawing a plan of your classroom, triggering and capturing memories of what happened there. Before you begin, you may wish to review the school memories you have already triggered. 🖐

Mapping Your Classroom

1. On a fresh sheet of triggering paper, begin to draw a simple outline of your classroom in whatever dimensions you remember it. Fill in the classroom plan with all the pieces of furniture you remember, in their proper places in the room: the desks (including the teacher's), windows, chairs, closets, supply closets, blackboards, radiator or stoves, bookcases, sinks, wall hangings, and so on. As you do this, capture any memories you are triggering, of people, events, and feelings. As before, write those key words at the exact location on the floor plan where you had that memory. 🖐

2. *Welcome back.* Now look at your drawing of your school desk, imagining yourself sitting there. Capture the key words for any more memories you will be triggering. Imagine yourself looking down at your desk. Are there any objects on your desk? Is there anything inside your desk, or underneath? 🖐

3. *Welcome back.* Now imagine yourself looking over the top of your desk toward the front of the room. Do you see your teacher and perhaps a child or children in front of you? Who were they and what are they doing? 🖐

4. *Welcome back.* Still imagining yourself sitting at your desk, turn to your left and then to the right, and repeat the same process. What do you see each time? Turn behind you. What do you see now? 🖐

5. *Welcome back.* Now review all memories of people

and things and events you have triggered and captured of the classroom of your youth. Do they include any school supplies you used? Was anything hanging on the walls, particularly near the blackboard? Was that teacher your favorite? If not, who was? Who were your special friends in that classroom and thereafter? And who did you not like? Why was that? What happened in that classroom? How would you describe your classroom experience to an important person in your life? If you're having any new memories, capture your key words. ✋

Using Your Memories in the Here-and-Now

Activities that you can do by yourself, and with friends and family

1. If you can, re-visit your old school. Bring a camera and your notebook. Ask for a favorite teacher. See if you can visit a classroom or the playground during recess, and be aware of what you are thinking and remembering. Study the children's faces. How is the school different than you remembered it?

2. Visit an educational supply house to see if you recognize any supplies you used as a child. Be sure to handle them and smell them. Do they smell or feel anything like they used to?

3. Share your memories with your partner, friends, family, and old school mates and see if your memories trigger any of theirs. Ask them about their school experiences and how they were different from yours. And if they were aware of what you have remembered, and whether they have different memories of events and people at your school.

While I worked on my classroom map, my mind suddenly flipped ahead in time to a memory of junior high school. My mother and I have been summoned into the principal's office to see what might be done about my recently uncovered *hearing* problems. Then my mind flipped backwards in time and this memory of me speaking –or rather, *not* speaking –in front of my elementary school class. Recreating that incident with as much detail as I could remember, observing the child I was from the perspective of an adult, seeing how I had overcome my "disability," convinced me of the healing potential of recovered memories.

The Making of an Editor

I see myself sitting silently and anxiously at my desk at P.S. 173 Manhattan. I had begun to stammer a few years before even beginning elementary school; weekend trips to a speech therapist on Fifth Avenue had not helped.

Now, I'm hyper-vigilant to the possibility of being called on, even though I had written a good paper. It's report time, and as usual, I avert my eyes from the teacher's as she looks around the room. I can't win this one: on the one hand, I'm afraid of being called on; on the other, I'm afraid that she'll read my evasiveness as my being not prepared.

This time my eye-slide doesn't work: I hear my name and am asked to come to the front of the room. Where is my next breath coming from?

I can see myself in front of the class now, looking out at them. The teacher is at my left, sitting at her desk. Does she know anything? Aware that I must avoid certain words if I am not to stammer, I read from my book report but edit the written report as I go, pronouncing the words silently to myself before saying them, avoiding for as long as possible (hopefully forever) those k's and m's and s's that would block my speech and turn me to stone. I rearrange and substitute the words to avoid those humiliating blocks and stutters, composing new sentences as I go. I become adept at finding synonyms. But sooner or later a synonym fails to appear, and a dreaded "corner," down at the end of the sentence, would become k-k-k-corner, a "said" would become sss-sss-said, a "mother," m-m-mmm-mother. Or, panicked entirely, usually when two or three difficult words were bunched together, I would stop altogether, scan the page with my head, and pretend to have lost my place in the report.

Much much later (much too late), someone told me that I could have said, "Hey, teacher, I can do this work but I have a terrible stammer and this isn't fun and I would appreciate not having to read my work aloud." But this didn't happen, so this mostly silent stammering continued through elementary school and far beyond, into my 40s in fact.

I don't stammer any more. In my 30s, I was surprised when I was angrily attacked for stammering during a job interview with a former stammerer (the man understood, as I did not, my anger that lay underneath).

The good news? Unconsciously, I used my disability as the foundation of one of the few careers I was able to have. I became a skilled editor of words, my own and others', and particularly adept at finding new ways to express new sentence constructions and meanings!

What Do *You* Remember?

Capture any memories you get as you answer these questions. Consider sharing your answers and your memories with friends and family, and asking them about similar experiences in their lives. Reflect carefully on each question before moving on.

1. Do you remember suffering from any "disabilities" or other problems as a child or young adult, and how you responded to them?

2. If you did, how did your parents, other family members and friends respond to them?

3. How did all of this affect your personality and your life? Did you overcome it? If you did, how did you do so? Are you proud of yourself?

Another Space in Your School

In this chapter, you will:

- Draw a plan of another space in your school –auditorium, playground, gym, etc.–and trigger more school memories

- Learn more ways to use your memories creatively, for self-understanding, and to improve your relationships with others

- Read other school memories that may trigger more memories of yours

I'm ten, and we're getting ready for a softball game, and I'm sort of watching myself. I know I'm good at batting, I know I'm a great pitcher, and still there's all this fear: Will I be chosen for the team? And when? Will I be chosen first, or right in the middle, or will I be the very last one? And If I'm the last one to be chosen, and I can bat and pitch and do all these things, what does everyone think is the matter with me? It all fleets through my head, and guess what happens? I'm the first one chosen. And then I wonder, why all the clatter in my brain? Is there something the matter with me? Every time I'm the first one chosen! And I always wonder...

–JOAN, 65

*Another reminder that you might want to get in touch with your breathing patterns right now, and **whenever** you begin a new exercise, like this:*

Deeply breathe in through your nose.

Hold your breath, then let it out slowly, through your mouth.

Do this several times, until you become more deeply relaxed and feel more energy available to be focused on what you are about to do. 🖐

This final school exercise will help you to remember significant experiences **outside** your classroom: perhaps in the auditorium; in the playground; in the lunch room, library, art room, locker room, or even in the principal's office. And perhaps remember any school-sponsored trips, like visits to museums.

Here are some triggering questions about some school-related spaces other than classrooms. Some will be easier to answer than others, but take your time. Capture any memories you are getting. If you trigger some memories that have nothing to do with the questions, capture them as well.

Before you begin, consider reviewing the school memories you have already triggered. 🖐

The Auditorium

1. Close your eyes for a moment, imagine yourself back in your elementary school auditorium, and open your eyes again. 🖐

2. Was anyone speaking from the stage? Was anyone singing, listening to music, watching plays or other school events? 🖐

3. Were you able to remember the auditorium? If you did, where were you in the auditorium? Did it have a distinctive scent? How would you describe that scent? Did you hear any music or other sounds there? Where were they coming from? Can you identify any music by name or hum some of the melodies? (At another time, the Source List in the Appendix could help you to identify some songs of your childhood.) Who else was there and what were they doing? 🖐

The Playground

1. Close your eyes again for a moment, imagining yourself back in your elementary school playground, and when you are ready, open your eyes. 🖐

2. Are you watching anyone? Are you doing anything yourself, like playing a sport or another game? Who are you with? 🖐

3. Do you hear any sounds in the playground? What are you doing there now? Who else is there and what are they doing? 🖐

Where You Ate Lunch

1. Again, close your eyes, this time imagining yourself in your elementary school lunchroom or wherever you ate lunch, and open your eyes when you are ready. 🖐

2. Are you in the school lunch room? Or did you eat lunch somewhere else? Who were you with? 🖐

3. Did this room have a unique scent? Try to hold that scent in your mind for awhile. Where did you sit wherever you had lunch? What were you eating there? Did you like it? Can you remember the specific foods you ate while in school and how you felt about them? 🖐

The Principal's Office

1. Luckily, not everyone will have this kind of memory. Close your eyes again for a moment, imagining yourself back in the principal's or assistant principal's office (if you were ever there), and open your eyes when you are ready. 🖐

2. How are you feeling as you think about the

principal's office? What happened there? Who else is there and what were they doing? Did you ever have a problem being disciplined when you were in school? What did it feel like? How did others respond? ✋

Using Your Memories in the Here-and-Now

Activities for you to do, and to do with friends and family

1. Do you (or your parents) still have any mementos from your elementary school days—yearbooks, programs, diplomas, awards, pins, artwork, drawings, and so on? Or can you locate any similar objects at a collectibles store or fair? Spend a little time with them and let your mind wander freely as you look at them.

2. Visit a nearby school playground and arrive during recess from classes. If you can, place yourself in a location where you can quietly observe what is happening with individual children, and also the patterns of the children's movements: how they move in and out of groups and who does what. Be aware, during all this, of what you are remembering and feeling. Be sure to bring your notepad for capturing any memories that are triggered.

3. For memories of another time period, adapt these exercises to another school in your life: another elementary school if there was one; high school; or college.

About these memories:
Once again, memories triggered at different times by different scents and here-and-now ▶ p. 83

Putting on the Brakes

It's early on in my school career, probably 2nd or 3rd grade. I'm sitting somewhere in the middle of the classroom, looking to my left to the window sill, admiring my bowl of flowering narcissus bulbs. Some time before, in one of the few annual rituals I can remember, the teacher brought a large box of narcissus bulbs to class, available to buy at five cents each. I got fifteen cents from my mother, brought three bulbs home. Then, as instructed, I put them in a brown paper bag and stored them on the upper shelf of the hall closet. At the proper time, they were removed and—roots had sprung! Now I would plant them in a flat bowl with pebbles and water, and later would bring them into class to show to the other pupils. I was so proud of what I had grown.

Decades later, the smells of narcissus flowers and bulbs is the sweetest smell of all to me. Although I miss the added odors of the dirty pebbles and rotting bulbs in that bowl, which I can't seem to recreate. Maybe one day I'll replicate it.

A memory of a classroom spelling bee:

Two single-file rows of children on either side of the classroom. It's a spelling bee, and I'm a really good speller, always have been. More and more kids drop-out. But I'm still standing. Soon it will be me and the dreaded Drucker twins. Girls. Very smart. And I'm getting anxious, and feeling what I would now describe as fatalistic.

As I correctly spell the new words, keeping up with the Druckers, I'm aware that I'm scared, that a part of me is holding back, although at ten or eleven I could never put the feeling into words, or talk about it. Yes, I'm not going to win. And one of the Drucker twins wins. I lose. Invariably. IN-VAR-IA-BLY.

Later, a flash of understanding:

Thinking about my school memories, I realize I was always ready to brake myself whenever I was faced

episodes are united in my consciousness for the first time. Taken one at a time, they are certainly interesting to me. But captured and related to one another (not by any thought process, but through the mysterious workings of the mind), they create new meanings and a clearer picture of the boy I was and the issues I continue to face as a man.

with a potential leadership or "success" situation. Number two was fine for me. My grades were predictably B+ (for Work) and A (for Conduct). I wanted to do well enough without being noticed, and in various ways would learn how to sabotage myself from going too far in my competitions with others, and with my accomplishments.

A related memory of a more recent event:

I'm in my 30s, and on my way home on the Long Island Expressway during a heavy rainstorm when an airport bus veers suddenly moving into my lane. Is there time to stop? I'm not sure. I see it coming and delay for a split second before applying the brake, and almost lose my life.

The final lesson—from my Toyota!:

I'm in my 60s, going down a hill in my home town, in a car that makes some noise when it brakes. The service people have told me that there's some dust in the linings and the car is safe though noisy. That's okay with me, but I am attracting some attention, which is making me uncomfortable.

A car quickly cuts in from a side street, just in front of me, and I need to apply the brakes. I delay, realizing that pedestrians on the sidewalk will be frightened and look disapprovingly at me. In that split second, I think that perhaps I should let myself hit the other car, but softly! And then I hear my mother's voice, saying, **"Now, don't make a fuss!" Don't call attention to us!"** I curse, jam on the brakes, frighten half the population of the neighborhood, and stop in plenty of time.

Later that morning I'm really angry, realizing (for the first time) that I don't have a single memory of any two people in our house having fun–really playing–with anyone else.

Maybe my parents had private moments of spontaneity, but I wasn't in that loop. As an only child, there was no one around full-time with whom I could play, wrestle, make music, share ideas, create imaginary scenarios and dramas, or be silly, joyful or competitive with.

What Do *You* Remember?

Capture any memories you get as you answer these questions. Would you consider sharing these and other memories with your friends and family?

1. As a child, how did you feel about competing with others, and about being a leader? Did you look forward to it? Did you shy away from it? Do you know why? ✋

2. What were the things you had a chance to compete about? And with whom? At home? At school? At play? How did your family feel about competition and rivalry? ✋

3. As you grew older, did your behavior change regarding competition? Do you now respond to competitive situations the way you did as a child, or differently? ✋

School Days

I'm ten or eleven, seated expectantly in the auditorium of Public School 173 with my class and a few others. We're there to appreciate great music. A teacher is playing 78 rpm recordings of classical music on an antique phonograph with a two-pound pickup and a coarse metal needle and it's glorious!

She's helping us to memorize some mnemonic aids so we can remember the tunes the next time we hear them. To a

Mendelssohn piano piece from "Song Without Words," our young, sometimes cracking, voices would sing: "Th-is is the Spri-ing song by Mendel-ssohn." And we'd sing other lyrics (that I'm sad to say I don't remember) to the music of Grieg and Dvorak and Schumann.

I had unexpectedly discovered what would become a life-long passion: my love of music and melody—as a listener though, not a performer.

■ ■ ■

Now, associating to the music appreciation classes, I'm back in the auditorium again, part of a chorus of Mickey and Minnie Mouses in some major production. We sort of dance. I am a pretty good Mickey, in full regalia, including a tail. My mask–it's woven out of some sort of scratchy stuff–hurts my face when I move in a certain way. During rehearsals, my tail keeps coming off and I carry it home to my mother for repair. I liked the smell of the whole thing and I remember the satiny touch of my Mouse pants.

■ ■ ■

Later, but still in elementary school, I'm receiving my Jewish education, and rehearsing for a group entertainment at the local Jewish community center. My job is to sing a popular song of the day: "Brother Can You Spare a Dime!" I do well enough with the refrain but cannot learn the verse well enough to satisfy the parent at the piano. She abruptly dismisses me and I leave the stage humiliated. I hate her for years but don't tell anybody.

Many years later, single again after many years of marriage, the incident rises to consciousness again. I'm invited to a large and unusual birthday party. To be admitted, everyone must do three or four minutes of something they did around the age of eight: do a dance, recite a poem, what-ever. A prize will be given for the best performance. I decide that I will re-enact and transform that painful old scene.

After a brief introduction explaining the background of my decades-old humiliation, I carry on an abrasive dialogue with the absent "pianist" and then get to sing the entire song. When it's over, I make an obscene gesture in the pianist's direction and walk triumphantly off the stage. The evening's prize is mine, and I'm judged as even better than the hostess, who as her contribution rendered a popular song from her parochial school days while performing a modest strip tease.

■ ■ ■

I'm going to my high school senior prom with Jean Darling, once an Our Gang kid, just a tad older than me, blonde and breathtakingly beautiful. I'm wearing a borrowed white dinner jacket I had borrowed from Shirley's Norman. Jean is wearing a gorgeous dress and a corsage that my mother had bought for me, and stored in the refrigerator just a little too long, so now it's wilted and I'm humiliated. Making matters worse, Jean snuggles against me when we're dancing (on the Astor Roof) and leaves lipstick on my borrowed jacket which I need to return to Norman.

What Do *You* Remember?

Capture in the wide margins or in your notepad any memories you get as you answer these questions. Consider sharing your answers and your memories with friends and family, and asking about similar experiences in their lives.

1. Did you ever wear a costume when you were little? What was the occasion? How did you feel about it? Can you remember what it smelled like? How it felt to the touch? ✋

2. Were you involved with music as a child, either at school or at home? Were you a listener or a performer?

The waltz does something to my heart. I'm moved in a way I cannot put into words.

—MICHAEL FEINSTEIN

_____

_____

_____

_____

_____

_____

_____

R.'s memory trigger: The sounds of the big bands, 1934-1941

_____

_____

_____

_____

_____

_____

_____

_____

_____

_____

_____

_____

_____

_____

If the latter, what instrument did you play? Did any friends, or anyone in your family, play a musical instrument? What feelings did you have about music then? What feelings do you have now? ✋

3. Can you remember–or have you already remembered–a humiliation of childhood? If you can, can you forgive the person who humiliated you? ✋

Your Childhood Home

In this chapter, you will:

- Draw a floor plan of a home of your childhood, triggering memories as you do

- Learn more ways to use your memories creatively, for self-understanding, and to improve your relationships with others

- Read memories of another's home that may trigger more memories of yours

The steps down to our basement always felt dangerous to me. I always had my eye on those steps to be sure no weird person would come down and kill me or something... Maybe I had seen a movie or...I don't know. But I'm still cautious about places I can't see into. It's not that I'm afraid of the dark, but of steps that I have to go down when I can't see ahead of me. I still don't like that.

–MARTA, 27

To relax before you begin, try breathing deeply, your own preferred way, or. . . .

Close your eyes, then imagine yourself experiencing your favorite fruit: an orange, an apple, or...

In your mind's eye, turn the fruit over and over in your hand. How does it feel to your touch? Bring it close to your nose? Do you smell anything? Bring it close to your mouth? Do you taste anything?

Be aware of any images or thoughts or feelings you are having. Begin the exercise when you're ready. ✋

Creating Floor Plans

1. Review your neighborhood map for a few minutes, focussing on your home and its surroundings, and capture the key words of any new memories that emerge. ✋

2. *Welcome back.* On a new sheet of triggering paper, begin to draw a floor plan, from a bird's eye view, of the house you lived in when you went to elementary school. If your house had more than one floor, use a separate sheet of paper for each floor. Map the outer dimensions of the house and then the interior walls of a single floor as you remember them, labeling each room you remember. You might wish to begin your floor plan at the front door. Capture key words of the memories you trigger as you do this— memories of people, furniture and other objects, and of events that happened there. Write your key words at the place on the floor plan where you remembered them. Don't rush; give yourself plenty of time before returning to the next step of the exercise. ✋

3. *Welcome back.* Now do the same for any other floors of your home, including the basement and attic. Continue to go slowly. When you have drawn floor plans and triggered memories for all the floors in this house. ✋

The Front Door

1. *Welcome back.* Now, on the floor plan of your childhood home, return to the front door. Imagine yourself walking through the door to the outside. Now imagine yourself standing outside the door, about ten feet away, looking toward your home. Can you remember the shape of the building? As

you stand there, imagine turning your head to the left, and then to the right. Can you remember the buildings or other areas around your home? Did anything important happen in or near those buildings? Capture any memories you are evoking. ✋

2. *Welcome back.* Now move to front door, open it, and go inside the house. Are there any familiar scents–or furniture, food, whatever. Go wherever your imagination leads you—to your bedroom, the kitchen, a secret space, or anywhere else. Are you aware of others in the home, and where they are? Move around the house for as long as you wish, capturing any memories you are getting at the place on your floor plan where you remembered them. Take your time. ✋

3. *Welcome back.* Now imagine yourself returning to the front door, opening it, and leaving your home, going out into your neighborhood. What did you see when you left your home? Nearby and in the distance? What season of the year is it as you look outside? Did anything important happen just outside the building or nearby? Re-read this and the other paragraphs if you need to. Are you having any more memories? Capture them. ✋

Using Your Memories in the Here-and-Now

Activities for you to do, and to do with friends and family

1. If you can, re-visit your childhood home, perhaps with someone else who is close to you. Stand quietly outside and focus your attention on it. Let the memories and feelings come. Consider approaching whomever is living there, explaining your situation to them, and asking them if you can enter briefly and look around. Bring your notepad or tape

recorder and capture any memories that emerge.

2. If the home is no longer there, stand near the place where it was and think quietly about it. Walk around the neighborhood. Try to find once-familiar neighborhood sites, and remember what you can. Capture your memories. Next time you are with someone who lived in that house with you, or visited it, share what you have remembered and ask how they felt about that house, and what they remember about what happened there.

3. Search through your family's photograph albums for any photographs of that home. At family gatherings, bring out the photographs and share information about what was happening when the photographs were taken, and anything else anyone remembers.

The Sporting Life

About these memories:
Some of these were triggered when I reviewed the memories triggered by my neighborhood map. They reminded me that my life was not entirely difficult. In fact, the triggering and re-telling of these childhood memories filled me with enormous pleasure and delight, and the boy I had been became even more familiar to me.

When I was really young, I ran a lot. In this memory, I'm running down the sidewalk on a hill in front of my house; I suck in my breath as I realize that I'm going too fast. My body is no longer at the correct angle to the ground. Oh. My feet begin to leave the pavement.

Now I have risen and am almost perpendicular to the ground, like a skier in flight (without poles).

Same scene, but I'm looking to my left, where several mothers are seated on camp chairs they have brought from their apartments on this hot summer day. Several of them stop whatever they are doing and look at me curiously, perhaps in horror. (I'm thinking: I know I have a meeting with the pavement, but how hard?) I'm wearing short pants!

I continue to face the mothers, who have now suddenly become an audience, one might say. I have moved my right arm under my head for protection as I land.

I come down heavily, my head lower than the rest of my body, and instantly produce on my right knee what will become another of my world-class scabs. I lay there, enjoying the situation. This is because several mothers have rushed over to help. I say, heroically, (Buck Rogers, Bobby Benson, Jack Holt, Tom Mix, rolled into one): "I'm okay." I feel absolutely wonderful.

■■■

My sporting activity was largely confined to the streets around my house, usually (for our roller hockey and slapball games) under the window of our third-floor apartment. My buddies and I rarely went to parks (other than the one across the street) or playing fields. They didn't feel quite as safe to me, and moreover were at the edge of our neighborhood, which as everyone knows is how far you can go before your mother gets nervous.

So we often threw footballs around or played touch in our street. Except for a short-lived football team we put together (the best part for me was getting my red-and-black jersey, including my favorite number, "33," the number of Cliff Montgomery, the Columbia University quarterback at the time). Actually, I'm not sure our team ever played anybody. Concrete felt like my spiritual surface; more amenable to my spirit than earth, which felt spongy, unfriendly, and somehow unsafe.

■■■

I played slapball a lot. In our version, it was played on a baseball-type of field, marked with chalk, between the sidewalks just under my apartment window, where mother would call me for dinner on schedule, at precisely five minutes of six, whatever might be going on in the game. Slapball seemed an elegant game: a high-precision non-impact sport.

I can still see myself at bat–"at hand," actually–tense, my

back to the Wall, Riverside Park and the Hudson River, my apartment building ahead of me, behind the pitcher, but barely noticed now. I'm ready to hit a pink high-bouncing Spaldina with my open palm, placing the ball between the infielders so I'd get a base or two. I was good at that. I needed to be aware, as I began my trip around the bases, of the bicyclists who would sometimes stray onto our field and collide with racing base-runners.

■ ■ ■

Some of our street sports were subtle, one might say elegant. Our six-story apartment buildings had, a brick's height from the sidewalk, very narrow ledges, perhaps a half-inch wide, probably an art-deco design element. The game was to throw a Spaldina or worn-out tennis ball against that ledge. Properly struck against the wall, the ball could sail two or three stories high, bounce off the building on the opposite side of street, hopefully avoiding entering a window along its way. As the ball returned to earth (the asphalt, actually), one bounce before caught became a single, two a double, and three a triple. Four bounces for a homer were, except against an inept opposition, rare occurrences. You could get a cheap single if you were willing to place the ball in the street rather than against the building. I was good at getting singles and doubles, and proud of my skill.

■ ■ ■

We played roller hockey in front of our apartment window too. I wasn't an adventurous skater—usually being more cautious than the situation required—but I loved throwing myself around in front of our chalk cage so no one else could score a goal.

There was one exception to my usual caution: I was fast and loved playing the backfield in pickup football games and getting dirtied and nose-bloodied. Often I ran straight into bodies just to feel the contact. At which point I

would consider the effect of my bloody nose on my
mother and quit the game.

■ ■ ■

Now I'm seriously sitting on the sidewalk, legs apart,
my feet in the gutter, a modified foot-long
Philadelphia Cream Cheese Box between my feet, facing
some potential marble players.

This was a game which may not have had a name. To play
it, you needed a mother who could influence their grocers
to contribute a wooden shipping box, about a foot long
and four inches square, that in the 20's and 30's was used
to ship those tin-foiled individual packages of Philadelphia
Cream Cheese—probably twelve to a box.

There were players and entrepreneur/concession owners. I
was in the latter group, using a hacksaw on the long side
of the box to create passages large enough to admit
marbles (immies?) of different sizes. Above each gate we'd
print the prize: "1" (more immie) for the largest and
easiest gate; "2" for the next most difficult; and so on. Get
a marble through the largest gate, end up with an extra
immie and of the same quality; get it through a smaller
gate, you'd do still better. Miss the gates (or box)
altogether and the concessionaire gets to keep the marble.

A young entrepreneur/concessionaire would sit on the
sidewalk, place the back of the box against the curb with
the passages facing into the street and wait for players,
who would stand behind a chalk line a specified distance
from the box. Chalk lines, as well as boxes and gate sizes,
varied.

Some players, taking the easy way out, focussed on the
largest gate; some did not. My particular skill was as a box-
maker: I carefully hack-sawed the openings so each was
just large enough to admit a marble of a precise size. So
my box was tough to play, but my prizes were greater, or

so I remember. I attracted the more competitive marble players, who of course evaluated the grade of each cheese-box course as if it were the 19th green at Pebble Beach. I did pretty well.

■■■

Between my apartment house and the Hudson River there was Riverside Park, which had many attractions, particularly after work began on vehicular approaches to the George Washington Bridge, only a block away. I liked to seek out what we called "izing glass" (actually a type of mica) whose layers could be peeled back and were as translucent as plastic. As we walked or talked, we peeled bark from small bushes.

Here comes a related memory of climbing inside a dark, damp place. When I was eleven, construction had finished on the bridge, and I would, terrified, but egged on by other boys, climb down the steep ladders attached to the inside walls of the foundation into the deepest, dampest depths of the bridge. Years later, I read a similar scene in *The Naked and the Dead*–an okay situation, except for a soldier's imagination–and was terrified all over again. I believed that, like that soldier, I would have fallen into the canyon.

■■■

As an adult, I'm privy to insights I never had as a kid: I liked to stop people (as an editor, I still do: stop folks from being unclear, ungrammatical, uninteresting); and I liked to be stopped (as a running back, enjoying being tackled more than running). I liked to get between places gracefully, as in slapball, and still do: I call it walking between the raindrops.

Remembering your own early experiences in sports–what you played and didn't play, how you played, your level of inner excitement and what got stimulated or upset by playing in a game, watching one, or even thinking about one, may teach you something about who you are today.

What Do *You* Remember?

Capture any memories you get as you answer these questions. Consider sharing your answers and your memories with friends and family, and asking them about similar experiences in their lives. Reflect carefully on each question before moving on.

1. What about your early life in sports? Do you remember something you achieved that you were really proud of? Or something you did that you were ashamed of? Did your parents or anyone encourage or discourage your participating in sports? Did your parents play any sports with you?

2. If you had brothers and sisters, what do you remember about playing with them? If you're a woman, did you participate in sports, and which ones? Did your family and school treat girls differently from boys around sports? How?

3. Which sports did you watch, and with whom? What fantasies did you have as you watched them? Who were your sports heroes or heroines? From your perspective as an adult, what characteristics of your childhood sports heroes or heroines do you think made them especially attractive to you?

(Recalling the bloop double that Gerry Coleman hit to win the pennant for the New York Yankees in 1949) *Oh, God, that cheap hit. It's like yesterday. It's like yesterday. It was the worst thing that had ever happened. That cheap hit. Forty years later I can close my eyes and still see it squirting to the line. Forty years later, it's all like yesterday.*

—TED WILLIAMS
Hall of Famer

J.'s memory trigger: Playing his favorite childhood game with his son

The Kitchen

In this chapter, you will:

- Draw a floor plan of an important kitchen of your childhood, triggering memories as you do

- Remember your favorite (and least favorite) foods of childhood

- Learn more ways to use your memories creatively, for self-understanding, and to improve your relationships with others

- Read memories of another's kitchen that may trigger more of yours

Some nights Mom would serve her meat loaf, covered with Del Monte Tomato Sauce and sliced green peppers. It was always served medium-rare. Before baking, she'd use a pencil to punch three evenly spaced holes half-way through the loaf and place ice chips in them, so the loaf would stay moist in the center!

–BOB, 67

Another way to relax before beginning to trigger:

Get yourself into a comfortable position and close your eyes. Then just scan through your body, seeking any place of tension. It might be your shoulder, your stomach, your back, or another place. When you come to a place like that, stop and imagine that this place of tension has a shape and color: any shape, any color. Then imagine a tiny plug at the bottom of that shape, with a little bucket right under it. And imagine pulling the plug, and just allowing all of the color contained in that shape to drain right out into the bucket below, overflowing to the ground if it needs to.

Stay in that quiet place for just a few minutes before beginning the exercise. ✋

In the next three exercises, you'll map three rooms in your childhood home: the kitchen, your bedroom, and another room of your choice. On your own, you can apply these same techniques to explore other home spaces that were particularly important to you: living room, bathroom, your parents' room, attic, basement, cellar, under the stairs, whatever. In the kitchen, you'll seek triggers not only in what you saw but in the childhood foods you smelled and tasted!

Mapping the Kitchen

1. Review the map you have already drawn of your childhood home. Focus your eyes and attention on the location of the family or community kitchen. Have your supplies ready. As always, don't begin before quieting your mind and your body, allowing room for the memories to appear. ✋

2. *Welcome back.* Once again, your map should be an overhead view, as if you were a fly on the kitchen ceiling, or a sharp-eyed bird in the sky overhead, looking through the ceiling to the kitchen below. Begin by drawing the outside dimensions of the kitchen. Was the kitchen square, rectangular, or an irregular shape? As you draw the kitchen, include all the objects you can remember. Draw slowly. As memories appear–of things, people, episodes– capture them. ✋

3. From a quiet place, perhaps closing your eyes for a moment, imagine you are a child again, standing outside the kitchen looking in. What do you see? Do you smell anything? Hear anything? Capture any new memories that emerge. ✋

4. *Welcome back.* Now imagine you are standing just inside the kitchen door, looking in. What do you see? (Give yourself plenty of time to remember.)

What do you smell in that kitchen? Do any smells linger? Is a meal being prepared that has a distinctive odor? ✋ Is a window open? Is there a fragrance emerging from the window? Close your eyes and see what else comes up. Capture your key words. ✋ On this page, write the names of those favorite and least favorite foods and meals you remember from your childhood. As you do this, include key words of memories that are being evoked.

More Questions About Your Kitchen

Welcome back. Now, taking your time, ask these questions of yourself and see if they trigger any memories. Read one question at a time, give any memories a chance to emerge, and then capture them in the wide margins or on your floor plan. Then move to the next question. ✋

- Where were the stove, the refrigerator, the cabinets, the table and chairs, if any? Where were meals prepared? Who did the cooking? ✋

- Where were the dishes, glasses, and cutlery kept? Can you remember any particular ones? Why do you remember them? Do you remember where they came from? ✋

- Did you eat in the kitchen? Always or sometimes? Who ate with you, and when? Did any important things happen while you were eating? ✋

- Were any parts of the kitchen particularly pleasant to be in? Were there some parts where you weren't allowed to stay? Or that you didn't like? What kitchen tasks did you participate in? ✋

- In your mind, can you smell anything as you revisit this kitchen once again? Do you smell any food or other odors? What wonderful or unpleasant tastes do you remember? ✋

Your Favorite (and Least Favorite) Foods

Again imagine yourself in your childhood kitchen, remembering those special meals that only your mother could prepare, and that only you liked–or disliked. Write the names of those favorite and least favorite foods on the table below. As you do this, capture key words of any memories that are being triggered.

Your memories may be of people or events that you associate to those special meals–perhaps at birthdays, holidays, or other celebrations. Running out of room? Use your notepad. If you remember foods or memories from other periods of your life, capture them also. Take your time, wait for a memory of food, and begin.

Breakfast	Lunch	Dinner	Dessert/Snacks

America's Favorite Foods

Here's a list of popular foods that others have remembered in triggering workshops. **Check** those or similar foods that you remember from your childhood kitchens. On the ruled lines or in your notepad, capture key words of any memories you are getting, of childhood or any other period of your life. Take your time, and return to the text when you're ready.

☐ A1 Steak Sauce _____

☐ Lea & Perrins
   Worcestershire Sauce_____

☐ Gulden's Mustard_____

☐ Quaker Oats _____

☐ Gerber's Baby Food _____

☐ Log Cabin Syrup _____

☐ Aunt Jemima's Pancake Mix_____

☐ Flour _____

☐ Corn Flakes, Rice Krispies,
   Shredded Wheat _____

☐ Holiday seasonings (like sage) _____

☐ Peanut Butter _____

☐ Honey _____

☐ Sugar cone_____

☐ Malt for malted milks _____

☐ Hot Fudge Sundaes _____

☐ Oreo _____

☐ Fig Newtons _____

☐ Chocolate Malomars _____

☐ Nabisco Sugar Wafers _____

☐ Hershey's Cocoa &
   Chocolate Syrup _____

☐ Nestle's Quik _____

☐ Jello _____

☐ Calumet Baking Powder _____

☐ Licorice _____

☐ Cracker Jack _____

☐ Popcorn_____

☐ Hershey's Chocolate Kisses _____

☐ Tootsie Roll _____

☐ Hershey's Chocolate Bar _____

☐ Jelly Beans _____

☐ Graham Crackers_____

☐ Kool-Aid _____

☐ Double Bubble Gum _____

Using Your Memories in the Here-and-Now

Activities for you to do, and to do with friends and family

1. Ask your parents (and grandparents) if they have any of your favorite childhood recipes. Borrow them and try them yourself. Invite family members or friends and share your likes and dislikes about food. If you have identified any foods or desserts you haven't had for awhile, try to find them again. Smell them, buy them, cook them, taste them. Do they evoke any new memories?

2. Next time you're at dinner with special friends, ask these questions: How did your family butter the corn when you were young? (Each person should demonstrate.) At dessert time: How did you eat an ice cream cone when you were little (from the top, licking or biting from the sides, or...)? Again, ask for a demonstration.

3. Ask your mother, dad or grandparent to cook a favorite meal again. While you're eating, share what you remember about old times, focussing on the meals in your house when you were young. Who ate with you? Was there always enough food? Does anyone remember the butcher, baker, and other shopkeepers and what they were like?

About these memories:
Beginning in the kitchen, my memories go back and forth in time, and I recall some lovely memories of food, my mother and my father—and another memory less lovely.

Kitchen Memories

A special treat was watching my mother bake her butter cookies. First she would complain about the uneven heat of the oven and about the landlord who did not honor his promise of replacement. Then, using a thimble covered with flour and occasionally dipped in water, she would dig a small hole in the center of the cookie dough.

Then, at the appropriate time (how did she know,

anyway?) she would interrupt the baking to place a dollop of raspberry jam in the center of each cookie. At the same time, she would also check their undersides and their degrees of doneness, the underside sometimes a light brown (most desirable) or no brown or at all, and sometimes brown almost to the point of burnt (good odor, not so good to the taste). Then back again to the oven.

■ ■ ■

I wasn't wild about leftovers, but they were served anyway, particularly day-old cooked spaghetti, dried out already from being in the fridge, baked in the oven with new sauce and dabs of butter added to the top ("Too dry, Mom!").

■ ■ ■

By now solidly middle-class and something of a sartorial dandy, my father had emerged from a struggling immigrant household on the Lower East Side of Manhattan. He had married "up." When I was young, he liked to cool his tea in the European manner, pouring it, little by little, into a saucer and drinking from the saucer. Whether or not this was his way of remembering and honoring his ancestors, it was not acceptable to my mother. Nor was his style of eating, which was to stuff a large amount of food in his mouth, and then seem to masticate it endlessly before swallowing.

■ ■ ■

At meals, I am always being asked to speak more slowly, in the hope that this would relieve my stammer, but I become more tense instead. I remember, at age sixteen or so, sitting around the dinner table with my parents, when my mother unexpectedly told me how she hoped I would be more successful than my father, and make more money than he had. I remember feeling stunned, and not breathing for a moment. I couldn't look at my father—

ashamed for him and for myself both. I waited for him to say something, but he didn't. I didn't either, and the conversation must have turned to another subject. I hated her then as I never had before.

What Do *You* Remember?

Capture any memories you get as you answer these questions. Consider sharing your answers and your memories with friends and family, and asking them about similar experiences in their lives. Reflect carefully on each question before moving on.

1. As a child, which foods did you like best? Do you still like them? Which foods did you hate? When the last time you had a childhood food that you really liked?

2. What were your mother's (or grandmothers', or aunt's) specialties? How did you feel about them? What were the foods you "had" to eat before you got dessert? How did you feel about them? Which foods did your mother and father (or other family members) like best?

3. What were the special treats you had outside your home—from stores or from other people's houses?

Your Bedroom

In this chapter, you will:

- Draw a floor plan of your bedroom in a home of your childhood, triggering memories as you do

- Remember your favorite toys of childhood

- Learn more ways to use your memories creatively and to improve your relationships with others

- Read several memories of another's bedroom that may trigger more memories of yours

When I was nine, I had this passionate love affair with Elvis Presley, in a blue bedroom with blue chintz flowered curtains. Well, there were sliding veneer mahogany closet doors–the big thing in the 50s–and the doors were always getting stuck on the track. Well (how much can you take of this?) I'd stand in the closet after opening the door, and use the wood frame of the closet and kiss it passionately, pretending it was Elvis. Then I'd go to sleep pretending that Elvis was with me, and that I had grown up and that he had waited to marry me. Actually, I was incensed because he had married a 14-year old girl. I mean, he only had to wait another five years for me, since I was nine. What a betrayal!

–SUSAN, 45

Still another way to relax before beginning to trigger:

Closing your eyes first, think of a place you'd especially like to visit again. A beach, a place in the mountains, a special room, a place you remember from your childhood, or recently visited on vacation. Or any other place that is important to you. Imagine yourself magically transported there. See yourself there, noticing what you're doing there, and remember as much as you can about what that place looks like, feels like, and smells like, before beginning the exercise. ✋

A Floor Plan of Your Bedroom

1. *Welcome back.* Once again, quiet your mind, your body, and your space, allowing plenty of room for the memories to appear. Have your supplies handy, together with the map of your home that you've been working on. ✋

2. Now review the map you have drawn of your childhood home, focusing on the bedroom. Then imagine yourself as a child again, standing outside the door of your bedroom looking in. What do you see? Do you smell anything? Hear anything? A radio? TV? Record player? Close your eyes for a moment, imagine yourself back in your bedroom, and open your eyes again. Do this now, and capture any memories you get. ✋

3. Now imagine you are standing just inside the bedroom door, looking toward a window or wall. Close your eyes. What do you see? Close your eyes for a moment, imagine yourself back in your bedroom, and open your eyes again. Capture those memories too. ✋

Creating a Map of Your Bedroom

1. *Welcome back.* Now draw a bird's eye view of your bedroom, capturing the key words of any memories that arise. Within your bedroom, sketch the location of the bedroom furniture as you remember it. Where were the bed, bureau, end tables, lamps, radio, TV, closets, windows, doors? Draw them all. Do this now and return to the text when you're ready. Take your time.

2. *Welcome back.* Review what you have just done. Where did you keep your dolls, toys, games, school books, hobbies, collections? Did you have a pet animal? What was hanging on the walls? What was in

the closet? Mark them all, capturing memories as you do. ✋

3. *Welcome back.* Again review what you have just done. When you have remembered an object–a toy, a doll, a game, a book, a hobby, a collection–try to recall how it felt and smelled. Did it have a distinctive smell, like a scented pillow, or a cap pistol after firing? Did it have a special feel, like a doll's dress or a baseball bat? Are you getting any new memories? Return to your floor plan now with these questions in mind, adding any new memories that are triggered. Take your time. ✋

4. *Welcome back.* This is a good time to transfer memories of your bedroom that are elsewhere in your collection–on your home map, in the margins–to the place they belong in the floor plan of your bedroom. Because you'll now have them in one place, new memories may emerge. Do this now. ✋

5. *Welcome back.* Now let's focus on you in the bedroom. How would you be feeling most of the time? Some of the time? And why? Were you ever in bed with an illness or injury? Probably. What illnesses or injuries did you suffer. What medicines or other remedies were you given, and where were they kept, in the bedroom or elsewhere? Do you remember their names, and, one by one, how they smelled or tasted? Do you remember what it felt like being in bed, while your friends were in school or outside, playing? On your floor plan, capture any memories or feelings you are getting. ✋

America's Favorite Toys (and their year of origin)

Let's return to your toys again. In the columns below, *check* any of these toys (or similar ones) you played with as a child. On your bedroom plan, capture any memories you associate to them. Also capture the names of any other toys you played with and other memories. (Some of these toys are so old they might stir up your parents' or grandparents' memories. Ask them sometime.)

☐ Parcheesi (1897) _____

☐ Flexible Flyer sleds (1889) _____

☐ Lionel Trains (1900) _____

☐ Crayola Crayons (1903) _____

☐ Teddy Bears (1903) _____

☐ Erector set (1913) _____

☐ Raggedy Ann dolls (1914) _____

☐ TinkerToys (1914)_____

☐ Lincoln Logs (1916) _____

☐ Yo-yo (1929) _____

☐ Lego Building Blocks (1930) _____

☐ Monopoly (1935) _____

☐ Little Golden Books (1942)_____

☐ Silly Putty (1945) _____

☐ Mr. Potato Head (1952) _____

☐ Scrabble (1953)_____

☐ Play-doh (1955) _____

☐ Frisbee (1957) _____

☐ Barbie dolls (1959) _____

☐ Hula Hoop (1959) _____

☐ Etch-a-Sketch (1960)_____

☐ Easy Bake Oven (1964) _____

☐ Spirograph (1966) _____

☐ Hot Wheels Cars and
Racing Sets (1968) _____

☐ Uno (1972) _____

☐ Dungeons and Dragons (1974) _____

(Courtesy of Toy Manufacturers of America, Inc.)

Using Your Memories in the Here-and-Now

Activities for you to do, and to do with friends and family

1. Ask your parents what they remember about your childhood bedroom. You might ask them: How neat (or messy) was my room? What was I like in those years? What things of mine do you remember? What did I like the best? Do you still have any furniture or other objects from my childhood? Can I see them? Ask the same questions of your brothers and sisters or whoever else lived with you. Encourage them to talk about their experiences.

2. Ask your parents whether they've saved any of your old things. If they have, get them and see what memories they trigger. Be sure to handle these things and smell them.

3. If you've remembered toys, dolls, stuffed animals, and other favorite objects from your childhood, you might create a weekend project of searching for them at antique and collectible stores and fairs. See if they trigger still more memories.

On Being Sick

I wake up in a strange bed, smelling over-starched sheets, surrounded by the color white, and screaming while arms and hands restrain me, voices try to calm me, and ice cream is forced down my throat. I'm two or three years old, and I've just had a tonsillectomy, a common procedure at that time, I was told, when a young child (and his mother?) suffered from his having too many colds. Shortly after the operation I begin to stammer, a practice I continued into my 50s. "You didn't like the ice cream?," my mother says, after being told this story, decades later. "You always liked ice cream."

■ ■ ■

At about the same time as I began elementary school, I had developed mastoids in both ears, and was operated on again.) Now I have a memory of going for a checkup at the doctor's office, in an apartment building between Fifth and Madison. I'm vaguely afraid, but I like going downtown on an open-top double-decker bus. For one thing, it's a "good" neighborhood, better than ours uptown on Washington Heights. The building has a doorman, and the doctor's office is reached not through the lobby, as in our building, but through a separate entrance accessible from the street. I like that.

■ ■ ■

I'm sick again, and nervous about being out of school, and about what I'm missing and could not catch up on. My mother has come in to "fix" the bed, setting me up in another room while she airs mine out and changes the sheets. After much too long a wait, I'm back in my room, and she tucks me in neatly, exactly in the center of the bed, sheets folded so tightly around me that I find it hard to move. What I want to do is to mess it all up, curl up under the sheets and pull them over my head, but I don't. (Today, when the sheets are made too tightly, I kick them off angrily before I can sleep.)

■ ■ ■

As I got better still I began to get solid food. The first meal would generally be boiled chicken mashed into dry potatoes. Or perhaps a poached egg mashed into the potato. This part of getting better felt like a punishment.

■ ■ ■

Now I'm sitting at my desk in first or second grade, carefully picking the long-healing mastoid scabs from the operation off my ears as they slowly turn wet and gummy. I dab them with a handkerchief. Somewhat disgusting to an outsider, I suppose, but it's all mine: the scum, the gumminess, the dripping.... The mastoid operations lead to a significant loss of hearing which is not diagnosed until I'm in junior high school. Like the stammer, the mastoids have a major effect on my personality unknown to me at the time.

What Do *You* Remember?

Capture any memories you get as you answer these questions. Consider sharing your answers and your memories with friends and family, and asking them about similar experiences in their lives. Reflect carefully on each question before moving on.

1. Do you remember any operations or serious illnesses you had when you were little? Or later on in life? Do you remember anyone else in your family having a serious operation or illness that had an effect on you or anyone else in your family?

2. How were you treated when you were sick as a child? Did you like the way you were treated? How did you "sooth" yourself when you were sick by yourself, or recovering from an illness?

3. Who came to be with you when you were sick, and what did you do together? Talk, play games, or... ?

The Glorious Smell of Books

I was shy and withdrawn as a child, and I read a lot, alone in my bedroom, the same books over and over again. One was *Pinocchio*, about a little boy whose nose grew larger every time he told a lie. Since my own nose was substantial, or so I thought, the book had appeal, although I never determined just what *my* lie was (later I decided it was unexpressed rage). Another favorite book was an illustrated

About these memories:

They were triggered not by an exercise, but by a visit to my favorite local bookstore. Browsing as I often do, I found myself attracted to a large gift book, printed on a rich glossy stock, like the

▼ p. 114

paper of my history books as a child. Wondering what the scent would be like, I opened the book, and lifted it close to my nose (was anyone looking, I wondered?). I smelled deeply (was anyone looking *now*?) and remembered my *Book of Knowledge* in its bookcase, and then related episodes of my youth.

I captured my key words on the small tape recorder I almost always carry. Later I would transfer them to a computer file, and finally elaborate them into stories. When I shared my stories with my wife, she said, quite happily, "I know you in a way I've never known you before." Our normal ways of communicating don't provide for such safe glimpses of the child that lives within all of us. When we share our memories with those we're close to, we can encourage them to share more of their own lives with us.

edition of *Peer Gynt.* A little later, sometime in high school, I would read Turgenev, and Dostoievky's *The Idiot.*

But it was the smell of the paper, the binding, and the covers that really got to me. My father had a cloth-bound edition of the Harvard Classics. I'm not sure I read many of them, but I sure did like the way they smelled. And I remember a set of classics from the New York Post and how *they* smelled. The truth is that I was as much in love with the way books felt and smelled as with what was in them.

■■■

At my little desk at P.S. 173 Manhattan, I'm really excited, although I'm not showing it. It's the beginning of the new term and brand new books, on coated paper, will be handed out. I know the teacher would not have enough new books to go around, and I'm hoping she'll remember that I had always taken particularly good care of mine, carefully mending bindings and pages when they were worn. I *deserved* to have a new one. If I got one, I would cherish and respect it, *never* turning up the corners of the pages to mark my place, and *never* carelessly leaving some droppings of a jelly sandwich over the pages. Sometimes I would even open them less often than I should have, not wanting to disturb the elegance or odor of those new pages! Sometimes I got the new books, sometimes I didn't.

■■■

The best thing, though, was going to my father's office on a Saturday morning. I was still in the early or middle grades of elementary school. He was an assistant manager at a district office of a large insurance company and never seemed to be finished with his desk work. At home, he would often sit at the dining room table, with his back to me, silently re-copying some ledgers, needing not to be interrupted.

Now he's in the office to clean up some more desk work. Except for us, no one else is there. But now I don't care that he's not paying attention to me, because I have something important to do.

I go into the company's stock room, a large airless closet that reminds me of a large stationery store! There are shelves upon shelves of blank ledger books, stationery, envelopes, writing pads, pencils, erasers, ink and inkwells—and all with the most distinctive scents!

But the surpassing thing was the stacks of newly printed booklets, for distribution to company customers and mostly devoted to health care. Because they were fresh from the press and had never been opened (or exposed to fresh air, for that matter), the ink was not quite dry and they were very aromatic! The content interested me too, as they were written very simply, in short words and simple sentences that even a small boy could understand. When I pick up a new booklet today, I sometimes find myself bringing it close to my nose before reading it. Even today, in my imagination, I can feel the smooth texture of that fairly heavy, lightly coated paper, and the precise aroma of that unique mixture of ink and new paper.

■ ■ ■

As I smell the paper in my mind, I remember something else. As I get older, and am obviously a serious reader, my parents purchase a brand-new set of the *Book of Knowledge*, which comes together with its own wooden bookcase. Now (or so they believe) I can browse through the world's knowledge in my own bedroom, and do research for my homework. But they underestimate the magic powers of touch and smell! The *Book of Knowledge* was printed on a gloriously scented, glossy, coated, heavy paper–something like the *National Geographic*—and I don't want to open them lest the delightful odors should escape! I mean I *would* open them in an emergency (if it were raining out, or I was not allowed to go the library) but mostly I sneak a sniff now and then, and do my homework research, as I always had, in the local library several blocks away, sitting on the floor, close to the smell of the stacks, probably not even reading what I had come for!

What Do *You* Remember?

Capture any memories you get as you answer these questions. Consider sharing your answers and your memories with friends and family, and asking them about similar experiences in their lives. Reflect carefully on each question before moving on.

1. Do you remember any books or stories from your childhood? Did any particularly influence you, and how? Did your parents read to you when you were small? If they did, do you have a memory of that, and how did you feel about it? How did they and others in your family–brothers, sisters–feel about reading?

2. What were your hobbies and what did you collect as a child? And what were your favorite objects as a child? Toys, blanket (blankie, moi-moi); teddy bear, doll? Where did you get these favorite things–as a present at holidays, birthdays, and other cele-brations; from your savings; as hand-me-downs? What happened to each of them?

3. What toys did you want and never got? Which toys did other kids have that you envied? What was your family's attitude about toys? How did your father feel? How did your mother feel? If you had brothers or sisters, how did they feel about your toys? (And how did you feel about theirs?)

Your Bathroom

In this chapter, you will:

- Draw a floor plan of your bathroom in a home of your childhood, triggering memories as you do

- Remember the scents and tastes of the medicines and pharmaceuticals of your childhood

- Learn more ways to use your memories creatively and to improve your relationships with others

- Read memories of other bathrooms that may trigger more memories of yours

In my grandmother's house, the bathroom had a window over the toilet which looked out over another apartment building and this bathroom always seemed a little creepy to me. I had this idea that if I flushed the toilet, which was very loud, a goblin face would pop up behind the bathroom window and scare me. So I would never flush the toilet! And everybody would be on me, and especially my mother, who was a clean-bug, to flush the toilet and I wouldn't. I never told them why. I was about four years old.

–SUZANNE, 55

Another way to relax before triggering:

Say to yourself the words for the five senses, one at a time. Stop after each one to see if any images or pleasant feelings emerge. If some do, capture them. And stay with your memories as long as you wish before beginning the exercise.

The five senses:

Touch 🖑

Sight 🖑

Hearing 🖑

Smell 🖑

Taste 🖑

Imagining Your Childhood Bathroom

1. Imagine you are a child again, standing outside the bathroom looking in. Slowly now... What do you see? Sink, toilet, mirror, cabinet, and... ? Do you smell anything? Soap? Toothpaste? Mouthwash? Cologne or perfume? Anything else? Do you hear anything? The sound of water or... ?

2. Now imagine yourself moving just inside the bathroom door, looking in. Was your bathroom square or rectangular? Where was the window or windows? What is on your left? Straight ahead? On your right? What do you see? When you begin to draw the floor plan of your bathroom, Be sure to put in all of those things, meanwhile capturing the key words for any memories you get.

Creating a Floor Plan of Your Bathroom

1. Begin to draw a bird's eye view of your bathroom. Within the bathroom's boundaries, include the location and names of the bathroom fixtures as you remember them. Where were the sink, mirror, cabinet, bathtub, under-the-sink cabinet, shower, toilet, towel racks? Do you remember where you kept your toothbrush and toothpaste, soap, and other things? Were pharmaceuticals and medicines kept here? What products were in this bathroom? Do you remember anyone else's belongings? Capture whatever you remember. 🖑

2. You washed and bathed here as a child, and perhaps dressed here also. Sometimes an adult might have been with you. Can you remember having baths or showers in that bathroom? How old is that memory? Did you like being alone in the bathroom? What's the nicest thing that ever happened there? Capture any memories you are getting. 🖑

3. *Welcome back.* Review the bathroom objects you have remembered–a particular soap, toothpaste, cologne, or perfume–and slowly imagine how each one felt and smelled. Did it have a distinctive smell, like soaps and toothpastes do? As you continue drawing your map, try to remember the scent of any other products, like ammonia, rubbing alcohol, mercurochrome, and iodine, that might have been kept in your bathroom? If you remember a medicine, can you remember (some people can) what it tasted like? Do those smells and tastes in your mind trigger any memories? Were there any toys in your bathroom? ✋

4. *Welcome back.* Do you remember any bathroom belongings of those who might have shared that bathroom with you. Parents, brothers, sisters, others. Were their things were different from yours—or did you use the same toothpaste, hairbrush, etc.? Add the names of those products and any other memories to your floor plan. ✋

5. Looking at your bathroom floor plan, imagine yourself standing at your bathroom door again, looking outside at whatever or whoever is facing you, perhaps on your way to your bedroom or some other room. What do you see? Capture your memories. ✋

Using Your Memories in the Here-and-Now

Activities for you to do, and to do with friends and family

1. Bring the list of bathroom products you triggered from your childhood to a pharmacy or supermarket and see how many of them are still available. (Perhaps the pharmacist can order a laxative or soap you used as a child. Buy something you haven't used

for many years. find a quiet place and open the containers, one at a time. Smell the contents, slowly. Taste the contents, when appropriate. You may be surprised at the flood of memories that results.

2. Share your triggered memories with those who lived with you at that time.

3. Explain the triggering process to them, inviting them to smell and taste the contents of your bathroom products and to share their memories with you.

The Weekend Pimple

With this memory, I jumped ahead in time, to early high school. Whenever I smell iodine or mercurochrome, I remember my nose. It seemed particularly generous and Cyrano-like when I was a child, at least until the rest of my face grew to catch up with it. Not surprisingly, I suppose, in my early years *Pinocchio* was my favorite book next to *Andy Blake in Advertising*.

Like most kids, I later suffered from acne. But mine was not your ordinary everyday kind, but on my nose.

During my high school years, when I was just beginning to date, every Thursday I would grow the hint of a pimple on the tip of my already prominent nose. It would rise slightly by Thursday. By Friday it would be full-blown, and the stress was beginning to build. Would it be gone by Saturday night? Or would drastic measures be necessary?

Has there ever been a cult film on the Return of the Killer Pimples? I mean, I had a date with Doris Brooks, who was blonde and beautiful. And I was aware (at some level, anyway) that Fred Astaire, Robert Montgomery and William Powell, my film heroes in those days, never seemed to have pimples in their scenes with Ginger,

Carole, and Myrna! Pimples, like bathrooms and double beds, did not exist in the films of those years!

Despite my attention, the pimple continued to grow, and by Saturday night was large and juicy. At my overworked mirror, I imagined I could see the activity going on inside of it. But if the pimple was thriving, I on the other hand was totally depressed. How could I be romantic under these nose-conscious circumstances?

I tried using mercurochrome and then white iodine to dry it up. No way. Once I covered the pimple and half my nose with a band-aid, claiming an accident of some sort, but the band-aid quickly fell off, revealing—the pimple! Nothing helped; the pimple seemed to have developed a personality of its own, stubbornly refusing to leave my face until Sunday night, when my dates were over, my opportunities ruined, and my next humiliation scheduled for the following weekend.

Now it's different. I don't have acne any more. My lovely wife, amused by this story, kisses my nose in tribute.

What Do *You* Remember?

Capture any memories you get as you answer these questions. Consider sharing your answers and your memories with friends and family, and asking them about similar experiences in their lives. Reflect carefully on each question before moving on.

1. Do you remember what embarrassed you most as a child?

2. Was this embarrassment about yourself or someone else?

3. Was it something about your appearance, or someone else's? Was it about something you did? Or something that someone else did?

The Sailboat

I'm very young now, playing in the bathtub with my sailboat and surrounded by the aroma of Lifeboy soap. The sailboat was wood, painted, possibly five inches long. I'd sail it back and forth in those soap suds, under the waves sometimes, and the back up again. Gradually the paint began to come off and the wooden hull slowly exposed itself. I helped it along, picking off the remainder of the paint with my fingernails. Soon I was playing with a wooden hull in the water. It was just as much fun.

Later, I remember having a toy cannon, a pool table, sulphur snakes, and a Buck Rogers Rocket Gun, but no one knew how important that sailboat was to me. Mother (for the third time): "Are you ready to come out?" Me: "No." At that point, Mom comes in to inspect my finger tips and finds them wrinkled from the water. The bath is almost over. A tad more stalling. I dock the hull in its regular berth, on the shelf in one corner of the tub, against the bathroom wall, and step out to be Mom-dried.

Although it's no longer available in my part of the world, I can still remember–in my mind–the exact fragrance of the orange Lifeboy soap I used as a child. Many years later I wonder, does any parent know how important a particular toy is to a child? Did I ever know how important their toys were to my children? Will they know how important their children's toys are to them?

What Do *You* Remember?

Capture any memories you get as you answer these questions.

1. What were your favorite objects as a child? Toys, blanket (blankie, moi-moi); teddy bear, doll? Where you got them—as a present, from your savings, as hand-me-downs? And what happened to each of them?

2. Do you remember the toys you got at holidays, birthdays, and other celebrations? And which toys you wanted and never got? And which toys other kids had that you envied?

3. What was your family's attitude about toys? How did your father feel about them? And your mother? If you had brothers or sisters, how did they feel about your toys? (And how did you feel about theirs?)

Escape to the Bathroom

Even though I lived in a big house, I never felt that I had much privacy. It was always a big issue for me. So when my sister and I got to go to summer camp for two months, from about 11 to 17, I just adored it. Smelling the pine trees. I loved playing baseball and being the best pitcher there. I loved playing tennis. And most of all, I loved my friends and my cabin. It was just the happiest and most joyful time of my year. And it was absolutely wonderful being away from my parents, just making my own way. Because there wasn't anything particularly compelling about being around that house anyhow. A lot of kids were homesick, but I wasn't, not for a minute.

"And I loved the lake that we swam in. It was beautiful and cool. We used to swim a mile and I was a really good swimmer. I loved to get in that lake and just go. I'd go out to the big rock, rest awhile, and then come back. That was a mile each way and by the time I was fourteen I was really up for it.

"Everybody cried when we left camp. Nobody wanted to leave, except the unpopular kids. We would all cry, and the counselors would cry; we knew that we would come back the next year, but that was ten months off.

About this memory:
This is my partner's memory—one of hundreds we have shared together—of returning from her summer camp. It was triggered by her bathroom map, accompanied by intense feelings, tape-recorded by me and then transcribed. Through triggering, we would know each other more deeply. An exciting way to animate and empower a relationship!

"And so I would come home and–I was never homesick at camp, but I was campsick at home!–I'd go into the bathroom where no one could see me, and I'd cry and cry and cry. Because I felt so displaced and so intruded on. I really didn't like it very much in my house."

What Do *You* Remember?

Capture any memories you get as you answer these questions.

1. Can you remember how it was to "re-enter" your home after being at another place you liked, or did not like, for some length of time?

2. As a child, did you share your room with anyone? Who? How did that feel? If you had your own room, did that situation change at any time, and how did that feel?

3. When you were growing up, was it possible to be private and alone in your house? Did you feel like you had to sneak away to be private and alone, or could you just walk away and feel that your wishes would be respected? How did your parents deal with your need to have privacy, to have spaces and things that were just yours, that maybe you didn't want to share with them or anyone else?

Our Bathroom Cabinets

With your floor plan handy, read this list of medicines and pharmaceuticals volunteered by members of a memory triggering workshop. All are more than fifty years old and commonly found in America's bathroom cabinets. Use it to help you remember identical or similar products that were kept in your bathroom cabinet.

Take your time, pausing after each product, writing the name of an equivalent product if you know, and–most importantly–waiting for memories to emerge. Capture your memories on the bathroom floor-plan, or in any other convenient place.

☐ Rubber hot water bottle _____

☐ Bromo-Seltzer tablets _____

☐ Castor oil _____

☐ Barbasol Shaving Cream _____

☐ Johnson's Baby Powder _____

☐ Fletcher's Castoria _____

☐ Ben-Gay _____

☐ Johnson's Foot Soap _____

☐ Lifeboy soap _____

☐ Luden's Menthol/Wild Cherry Cough Drops _____

☐ Phillips' Milk of Magnesia _____

☐ Pepsodent Tooth Powder_____

☐ Dr. Smith's Cough Drops _____

☐ Robitussun _____

☐ Band-Aids_____

☐ Ex-lax _____

☐ Cotton swabs _____

☐ Pepto-Bismol _____

☐ Jergen's Lotion _____

☐ Old Spice After-Shave _____

☐ Mustard plaster _____

☐ BAN _____

☐ Vaseline _____

☐ Lavoris _____

☐ Vicks Vapo-Rub _____

☐ Ammonia _____

☐ Rubbing alcohol _____

☐ A freshly opened bandage _____

☐ Iodine _____

☐ Mercurochrome _____

A Special Place–At Home or Away

In this chapter, you will:

- Draw a floor plan of a special place of your childhood–either at home or away from home–triggering more memories as you do

- Learn more ways to use your memories creatively, for self-understanding, and to improve your relationships with others

- Read memories of others' special places that may trigger more of yours

You remember the Andrews Sisters! Big vocal group of the 30s and 40s? Sang with Bing Crosby. I was around five or so, and I hated them. It seemed like my mother and father were always in the living room, playing their darn record of "Bei Mir Bist Du Schoen," dancing and hugging... I still get upset when I hear their records. I was so jealous!

–ANNGWYN, 48

*Another way to relax
before beginning to trigger:*

Find a favorite recording
of music from your
childhood or any other
period of your life. (You
may have one in your
house, or might find one
in a nostalgia, oldies,
rock, or easy listening
section of a record shop.
The Source List in the
Appendix (page 193)
suggests places to look.)
Play the music softly,
with your eyes closed,
before you begin the
exercise, being aware of
any thoughts, images, or
feelings you are having.

———————————

———————————

———————————

———————————

———————————

———————————

———————————

———————————

This next floor plan of another room in your house is your choice. It might the place where your family during those school years would be likely to spend time together–perhaps a living room, family room, TV area, den, or... ?

You might also choose your own special place–attic, garage, secret hiding place–or a place away from home where your family spent days off or longer vacations together. It might be where you visited other family or your friends, or where you went shopping or to sports or entertainments. It's your choice. Spend some time thinking about the place you will map and then return. Take your time. ✋

Drawing a Floor Plan of the Place

Once again, quiet your mind and body, allowing room for the memories to appear. Have triggering paper and your notepad handy, together with the map of your home that you've already completed.

1. Now review the map you have drawn of your childhood home, focusing on the place you have chosen. Imagine yourself as a child again, standing outside the door of this new place, looking in. What do you see? Do you smell anything? Hear anything? Close your eyes for a moment, imagining yourself again in this place, and open your eyes when you are ready. Do this now, capturing any memories you are getting. ✋

2. *Welcome back.* Now imagine you are standing just inside this place, looking toward a window or wall. What do you see? Hear? Smell? Can you imagine yourself touching anything? Close your eyes for a moment, imagining yourself again in this place, and open your eyes when you are ready. Do this now,

capturing any memories you are getting. 👋

3. *Welcome back.* Now draw a bird's eye view of this
   place, including not only its boundaries but windows,
   doors, wall hangings, and furniture as you remember
   them, including key words as you do. 👋

4. *Welcome back.* Return to your drawing and include
   the location of other objects you remember in this
   place. Some will be visible and others not. Some will
   be your special favorites. Did anything in this place
   have a particular sound or smell? Did anything feel
   good to the touch? Include whatever you remember,
   capturing your memories as you do. Do this now
   and return to the text when you're ready. Take your
   time. 👋

5. *Welcome back.* Now review what you have drawn,
   focussing on any people who were in that place with
   you? What did you do there? By yourself, and with
   others? Imagine yourself behaving in the way most
   typical of you. What were you doing? How were
   others in this place responding to you? Capture any
   memories that are emerging. If you are triggering
   more memories, capture your key words on your
   floor plan. 👋

Using Your Memories in the Here-and-Now

Activities for you to do, and to do with friends and family

1. If the place you chose was a family place, ask your
   parents what they remember about it. You might ask
   them: What was I like in those years? What did I
   like the best about this place? Do you still have any
   furniture or other objects from there? Ask the same
   questions of your brothers and sisters or whoever
   else lived with you.

2. Share with your family any memories you have of a secret place that they didn't know about–in your house or outside–a place where you went at special times?

3. If you've remembered any objects you particularly liked in that place, you can create a project of searching for them at antique and collectible stores and fairs. They may trigger more memories.

Going Out

Mostly we ate at home, but my parents liked to eat out—Chinese food, then very unimaginative, but my Dad (impressing me) always ordered extra slices of white-meat chicken on top, and my mother always wiped the silverware with a napkin while I always looked to see if the waiter was watching. At the major sea food restaurants in and around Manhattan, we ate the best in sea food— lobsters, oysters, clams; and prime steaks by the pound at out-of-the-way places in Manhattan's industrial districts. I liked being with them then, and have always been grateful to them for introducing me to a variety of food.

I especially waited for those times when we went to my favorite restaurant because the waiter brought the soup in a thick metal cup with a handle–a "porringer"?–and poured it ever so carefully into the bowl. This was a special and eagerly awaited treat for me, but my mother (as usual) had a different memory when I recounted mine: she remembered that I liked that restaurant because the bathroom was so clean.

■ ■ ■

One day–this was rare–a young friend invited me to dinner at the house of a relative. I'm sitting awkwardly and silently at the table and notice the host putting *black pepper* on his peas! This was fascinating! I began to do it. I still do it.

■ ■ ■

On an overnight to my "Cousin" Irwin at my "Aunt" Claire's apartment, for dinner we have, instead of a salad, *cold brains* on a lettuce leaf. Did I eat it? I hated it, but "Aunt" Claire insisted it was healthy. Later Irwin and I have a pillow fight in his bedroom. Today brains is (are?) one of my favorite foods. So how do you figure?

■ ■ ■

I am even younger, and on a rare visit to my Aunt Rose's apartment. She is my grandmother's sister; her husband Phil is wealthy, in real estate, and a family benefactor, as I learn much later. I am standing outside a black wrought-iron gate which is locked, and protects the living room from unwelcome visitors. Inside the room, I see sashes stretched across the chairs, to discourage sitting even if one could get inside. I remember those sashes years later during my visits to the Frick Museum in Manhattan. In the way that we often stereotype and caricature people through the lens of their eccentricities, this is all I remember about my Aunt Rose.

What Do *You* Remember?

Capture in the wide margins or in your notepad any memories you get as you answer these questions. Consider sharing your answers and your memories with friends and family, and asking about similar experiences in their lives.

1. Do you remember any special outings with your family? What you did? Who was there? What was

the most exciting thing that happened?

2. Do you remember going out with your friends? What you did, and what was special about it? The most exciting thing that happened?

3. Do you remember going out by yourself–for adventure, excitement, or... ? And how you felt? What was the most exciting or terrible thing that happened?

About these memories: All three were triggered by the Places exercise, and all occurred at different periods in my life. Brought together, they helped me to understand for the first time their relationship to one another, and how they exemplify my life-long issues about competition. This is an example of memory triggering as a teacher.

About Competition

I'm still a kid, maybe eleven or twelve. It's vacation time, and my father has not yet appeared for his weekend at the summer resort in Moodus, Connecticut. I'm enjoying myself, and my mother likes this place too. Counselors (probably high school students, but Authority Figures to me) would take us over for the most of the day. On a cow pasture near the main buildings, my counselor has put together a baseball game.

I'm playing outfield, either right or center field. A fly ball is hit toward me, to my right, and I run for it. I'm a fast runner, and approaching the ball, begin to stretch out my body and my glove arm, not sure whether I can reach the ball or not. At the last instant, reaching for the ball, I step into a badger hole. I begin to fall, and the ball goes into my glove. The counselor comes running out to see if I'm okay, then congratulates me on the catch. This was my all-time highlight in the world of sports, remembered again and again through my youth, never again duplicated or exceeded.

■ ■ ■

In high school, I try out for the De Witt Clinton football team. I'm fast and I've got good hands, so I can catch passes. I make an exceptional catch and a coach notices me. He says to someone, "Let me see that kid again." Or something like that. Aware that he's watching me, I run a pattern, the ball seems overthrown and to catch it I'd need an extra burst of speed and a good stretch. My body becomes tense, I don't try, and I don't reach the ball. The coach turns his attention elsewhere, and something within me is not surprised.

■ ■ ■

A little later in time. I'm playing touch football in Central Park with my best friends. Because I'm fast I'm chosen to receive the kickoff, which I await with a strange mixture of excitement and dread. The feeling is familiar to me, meaning something like, first, "This is going to be good, and then, "It's not going to be good after all."

I make a good catch, run to my right, and gather speed. Then, as I become aware that tacklers are approaching me, I'm also aware of deliberately slowing down. I am tackled. No breakaway, no touchdown. Later one of my buddies tells me, "We know if you don't get into the open field, we can always stop you." Now I'm depressed. Much later, I learn that for most of life, this was my story.

What Do *You* Remember?

Capture in the wide margins or in your notepad any memories you get as you answer these questions. Consider sharing your answers and your memories with friends and family, and asking about similar experiences in their lives.

1. Did you achieve something in sports that you were really proud of? Or ashamed of? How did you feel about winning? Losing? What were your sports highlights?

2. Which sports, if any, were valued in your family?

Did your parents encourage you to participate in sports? Did anyone else encourage you? Did your parents play any sports with you?

3. Which spectator sports did you watch? What did you like best about them?

4. Who were your sports heroes or heroines? What do you think made them especially important to you?

If you had brothers and sisters, what do you remember about playing with them? If you're a woman, what was it like to be a girl and compete in sports? Were the girls in your family and at school treated differently around sports from the boys? How?

The Elevator

My childhood nightmare. I'd have it (and countless variations) over and over again.

I would enter our apartment house elevator, take it to our apartment on the third floor, get out, take a sharp left, then a sharp right, to the door of Apartment 3-C, which was ours. This was what I did, actually, every day, several times a day.

Our elevator, like many others in those days, had see-through doors, so as you rose you could see the floor numbers painted in foot-high type just under each landing. So I'd see "2" and then "3," a short trip and then I'd be there.

In the dream (while my observing mind–that part of me that was still awake–told me this was going to happen again!) the floor numbers appeared out of sequence as we rose: 2-4-6-5-1 and so on, but never 3, where I was supposed to go. Instead, the elevator would continue and continue to rise, higher than our 6-story building.

Finally the 3rd floor would appear. I would get off,

relieved and still frightened, and walk to my apartment, which turned out, after I managed to get my key into the lock, not to be mine at all, but someone else's, with everything in the wrong place.

I dreamed this dream over and over again, and it terrified me every time.

During the days though, I felt contented, as if everything was as it should have been, except for a sadness or melancholy as I walked home at the end of a school day, particularly on turning-dark autumn and winter afternoons, or after running late-afternoon errands for my mother.

What Do *You* Remember?

Capture any memories you get as you answer these questions. Consider sharing your answers and your memories with friends and family, and asking about similar experiences in their lives.

1. Do you remember any dreams or nightmares you had as a child?

2. Do you know now (or did you know then) what might have stimulated them?

3. Did you ever talked about them with anyone? Do you continue to have any old dreams or nightmares today?

I took great care to try to understand every single image...and, above all, to realize them in actual life. That is what we usually neglect to do. We allow the images to rise up, and maybe we wonder about them, but that is all. We do not take the trouble to understand them, let alone draw ethical conclusions about them. Failure to understand them deprives (one) of wholeness and imposes a painful fragmentation on life.

—CARL JUNG

C.'s memory trigger: The scent and touch of Ivory soap triggered memories of her children as infants, and of her childhood home

Important Places of Your Life

In this chapter, you will:

- Create a list of places where you have lived throughout your life, triggering more memories as you do

- Focus on remembering one place that is particularly memorable to you

- Learn more ways to use your memories creatively and to improve your relationships with others

- Read memories of others' important places that may trigger more memories of yours

In junior high, my friend Kim talked me into signing up for cornet lessons with him. There was one big drawback, though. In the high school music room, where the lessons were to be, water from spring rains seeped through the old foundation like a sieve. When we arrived for our first lesson, our music teacher handed each of us a mop. He said he couldn't teach us to play with three inches of water on the floor. By the time the floor was dry, the period was over, and three clarinetists were waiting at the door for their lesson. It rained a lot that spring, and every Monday our lesson went the same way, and we'd return home without blowing a note. After several weeks of non-practice for non-lessons, I decided I was not destined to play the cornet. But Kim was determined to carry on, and somehow, before long he was playing in the school band.

–BOB B., 55

With these next four exercises we leave the world of elementary school to use new ways of triggering memories of other periods of your life. You'll use the same triggering guidelines as before, and the same supplies. **Be certain to quiet your mind, your body, and your space before you begin.** When you're finished, you'll have a reservoir of key words and memories that covers the entire span of your life, together with several ways of creating a permanent record of your memories that you can share with your family and friends.

Places of Your Life

(In the margins, capture any memories you are getting as you read these instructions.)

In a few minutes, you will begin to create a list of all the addresses where you lived or spent extended or other significant time during your life. These will include your homes over the years, and perhaps the homes of certain relatives or friends. Besides places where you lived, include other addresses that have special significance to you: perhaps important work places; a live-in or commuter school; a church or temple; a hospital if you have been seriously ill; a gym or stadium if you are an athlete or fan; a concert hall, rehearsal hall, or theater if you are a musician, performer or fan; a studio or museum if you're an artist. Any place that comes to mind may be important enough to produce memories, whether all the details are immediately available or not.

Creating a Master List of Addresses

1. For this exercise, you will need at least five sheets of your 8-1/2 by 11 paper. Begin by dividing the five pages into two vertical columns, labelling the left-hand column "Places" and the right-hand column,

"Memories." Do this now and then return to the text. As always, take some time to liberate your physical space from any possible distractions. Quiet your body as well, being aware of your breathing to help focus your energy. Do this now and return to the text when you're ready. ✋

2. Beginning in the first "Places" column and continuing until you can think of no more important addresses, write the first address of your life, if you know it, and then capture any other addresses that are evoked, in any order. Be as detailed as you can: street address, city, the years you lived there, your ages at the time, If you have forgotten some addresses and if some occur to you out of chronological order, that's perfectly all right. ✋

3. As you identify these places, accept whatever comes into your consciousness, allowing yourself to associate memories to those places freely, without judging the importance of a particular place or memory. Write those memories in the "Memories" column. Use as much paper as you need, and don't worry about neatness. Now begin whenever you're ready, returning to the text whenever you're ready. Take as much time as you need. ✋

Welcome back. You may wish to stop for awhile before beginning the next part of this exercise. When you're ready, move to the next step, where you will focus on a single place, and then other places if you wish.

To relax yourself before beginning to trigger, try breathing deeply, use your own preferred way or. . . ?

Find a family photograph album, the older the better, and allow your eyes to gaze lazily over the photographs, being aware of any images, thoughts or feelings you are having. Capture them. Then begin the exercise.

Focussing on a Particular Place

1. *Welcome back.* Again have several sheets of your triggering paper handy. As always, take some time to liberate your physical space from any possible distractions. Relax your mind and body as well. Do this now and return to the text when you're ready. ✋

2. *Welcome back.* Now, from the master list you have just created, the one place that you are most excited about exploring right now. (It's usually a good idea to go with your first choice.) Then return to the text. ✋

3. *Welcome back.* On a blank page, in the top right-hand corner, first transfer all the specifics you remember about the place you have chosen: the address as accurately as you know it, the years you were there, and your approximate ages at the time. Then transfer whatever memories about this place you have already evoked in your master list. As you're doing this, associate freely to the address and the memories, capturing any new memories that emerge. (You can expect several.) After you've done this, return to the text. Take your time. ✋

4. *Welcome back.* Now, if you wish, transfer all the memories about this place you have already triggered through other exercises (on maps, floor plans, notepad) to this same sheet. Do this, taking your time, and return to the text. ✋

5. Now slowly review the questions on the opposite page, triggering and capturing more memories as you do. Take your time. Finally, apply all these techniques to any other important places of your life.

Questions You Might Ask About Each Place

Think about these questions as you explore each place. Refer back to them as often as you need to.

1. How did this place fit into the physical space around it? Was it in a town or city? If so, what neighborhood was it in? What street or road was it on? If the place was in a rural area, what were the surroundings like? Stop now, think about the place, possibly closing your eyes for a moment. Underneath the place description, capture any memories that emerge. ✋

2. Imagine now that you are outside that place, staring at it. Study it carefully. How was the building constructed? Did anything happen on the sidewalk or land outside? What season of the year is it now? Again, think about the place, possibly closing your eyes, and capture any memories that emerge. ✋

3. Imagine yourself inside the place. Did it have a distinctive odor? Walk through the rooms, taking your time as you go. What is there? Who was there with you? ✋

4. Imagine yourself in the room where you spent the most time. Can you recognize any furnishings or other contents? Some things you particularly liked may be there. What were they? Were any family or friends likely to be there? Did you hear any special sounds here? Was there anywhere else in this place where you then wanted to be, or would now like to be. ✋

5. Was there a kitchen in this place? If there was one, imagine yourself there. Does the kitchen have a particular odor? How would you describe it? What kind of food did you eat in this kitchen? Who would you be eating with? What does it feel like living in that house with the people you are living with? ✋

6. Was there music anywhere in this place? Where is it coming from? What is playing? Can you remember the melody? Can you remember the words, if any? Would you like to hear it again? Are you having any memories? ✋

7. Now go somewhere in your place–perhaps at a window or door–where you can look outside. What did you see as you looked outside? What was happening? What did the air feel or smell like? What was the temperature? ✋

_____

_____

_____

_____

_____

_____

_____

_____

_____

Using Your Memories in the Here-and-Now

Activities for you to do, and to do with friends and family

1. Are you still able to visit any of the important places of your life? If you can, visit them, as well as the immediate surroundings, and capture your memories. Later, you can add your place memories to the memories you have already triggered.

2. When you find a place where you lived, worked, or played, you might try to get inside. If it's a place where you lived, sometimes a knock on the door and an explanation of why you're there will trigger an invitation from the current tenants or owners for you to walk around the place. Capture any memories that you get.

3. Create a list of people you knew during the time you spent at these places, together with any memories you have of them, and of what you did with them. If those people are still accessible, share your memories and ask them what that experience was like for them.

About this memory:

As you become more aware of memory triggers in your environment, you may consciously seek them out and *use* them; for example, I have searched for (and smelled) my mother's perfume and my favorite flower, and searched for particular musical recordings from my childhood or adolescence that I suspected would trigger me. ▶ p. 143

Furniture on the Sidewalk

His name was Bobby Wayne, and he was special to me. We hung out together for many years, without saying very much. I think he was a sad boy, and very smart. He wasn't Jewish like I was, and for some reason I did not try to understand, I always felt a little awkward around him. I don't think I ever met his parents, or ever was in his house (he may not have been in mine, either) and I know now that they were probably poor.

He lived around the corner, and he was with me on one of the big days of my life: the day I learned to whistle, when I was six or seven.

Bobby and I were running down the back stairs of my apartment building, fast, not wanting to wait for the elevator, and for the thousandth time, I'm trying to whistle properly. Suddenly I get it, and as excited as I've ever been in my life, I run back all the way back upstairs to demonstrate what I've learned to my mother.

Years later, I come home from school to find a family's furniture on the sidewalk outside of Bobby's apartment building. Someone tells me it belongs to his family and that they have been evicted. I see people moving within the cluster of furniture and soon realize that they are Bobby's family but I keep my distance. I don't know what to do. (I don't think of asking my mother, who is probably upstairs, what to do. If I had, she probably would have said, "Don't get involved. It's not your business.")

I see that Bobby has joined the family group but I don't go over to him. I'm ashamed—for him, for his family, and then finally for me. And then they are gone, and I never see him or hear from him again.

What Do *You* Remember?

Capture in the wide margins or in your notepad any memories you get as you answer these questions. Consider sharing your answers and your memories with friends and family, and asking about similar experiences in their lives.

1. Have you ever had a friendship where you felt both closeness and distance, perhaps separated by social class, religion, or age—a friendship conducted in isolation from the mainstream of your life?

2. Did you ever feel sad, ashamed or regretful about events you felt you could not, or did not want to, control? Or where you did not know what to do or say? When did this happen? Where? With whom?

3. Did you ever want to reach out to someone and not be able to do so? Tell yourself a story about it. Can you tell your story to someone else?

After unexpectedly remembering something, you may search your memory of the immediate past to see what might have triggered that particular memory (was it the smell of those pine cones, that soap, that music of the 40s or 70s, or... ?) This memory was triggered by my reading of William Maxwell's *So Long, See You Tomorrow*, a few weeks before I created my neighborhood map.

Key Events in Your Life

In this chapter, you will:

- Create a list of key events in your life, triggering more memories as you do

- Focus on key events at one particular place

- Learn more ways to use your memories creatively, for self-understanding, and to improve your relationships.

- Read memories of others' key events that may trigger more memories of yours

When I was eight and for four years after that, I danced in the "The Nutcracker" with the San Francisco Ballet: under Mother Goose's skirt, and then as the rear legs of a dragon, and finally in costume in the ballroom scene. I loved it all: being greeted by the guard I went through the stage door; walking every inch of the backstage area— the dressing rooms, the prop room, the catwalks. Going through the halls and beautiful staircases of the Opera House. Those cold hard floors under my soft ballet shoes! And wearing my Mom's kimono, just like the ballerinas! Being so quiet backstage. And then watching the rest of the performance from the percussion area. Hearing that lovely music LIVE! Leaving the stage door with my makeup on and hearing people say, "Look, she was in "The "Nutcracker." Actually, the performance wasn't all that important but everything else was!

—MARCELLA, *36*

Questions About Key Events

At an important place or during an important period of your life:

Did you, or anyone close to you, experience outstanding personal achievements? ***What are your memories? Capture them.***

Did you, or anyone close to you, experience an outstanding financial success? ***What are your memories? Capture them.***

Did a family member leave or return home (because of school, a job, a marriage, military service, a divorce, etc.) ***Continue to capture your memories.***

Did you, or anyone close to you, marry?

Did you move to a new home?

Were there major changes for anyone at work (getting a promotion, losing a job, etc.)

Did anyone important to you retire or stop working for some reason?

Were there major changes in your family's living conditions?

Was a parent or anyone close to you involved in a divorce?

Was there was a reconciliation or separation?

Did you, or anyone close to you, suffer a serious illness or injury?

Did a parent, close family member or friend die?

What are your memories? Capture them.

Were there serious arguments in your family?

Did anyone have alcohol, drug, or emotional problems?

Was there trouble with friends or neighbors?

Have you ever had an experience that you did not fully understood at the time, but now understand affected you very deeply?

All of us experience key events in our lives, major or minor, pleasant or unpleasant, simple or complex. After key events, our lives turn in different directions, and are never quite the same again. Going off to school for the first time, finding or losing a loved one or a job, getting married, and moving to another city are all commonplace examples of key events. Others are less common, like winning a sweepstakes or inheriting a fortune. How would you identify your key events? And what memories are associated with them? To discover both is the plan of this exercise.

Memories of our key events can be potent touchstones for self-knowledge and particularly powerful tools for communicating with others, because others have similar if not identical experiences, and will often be interested in hearing ours as we may be interested in theirs. Who, for example, has not had a romance, achievement, or disappointment that has not changed her or his life? Memories of similar experiences can encourage us to talk more intimately with one another.

(About food critic MFK Fisher) *She captured the dawn of adolescence in her first taste of oyster. Slurping the bivalve at a dance at her all-girl boarding school, She wrote, "I swallowed once, and felt light and attractive and daring." Just then, an older girl pulled the young epicure into a slow dance, and the feel of the oyster slipping down her throat was forever tied to the ensuing panic and intrigue.*

—Molly O'Neill in the *New York Times*

Identifying Your Key Events

1. You'll need your usual supplies and your collection of triggered memories. Begin only after you have quieted your mind, your body, and the space where you will trigger. It's probably best to use your 8-1/2 by 11 inch triggering paper for this exercise. ✋

2. Divide several sheets of your 8-1/2 by 11 inch paper into two vertical columns. Label the left-hand column "Key Events" and the right-hand column "Memories." Capture, in no particular order, any key events in your life that come easily to mind, together with any memories you associate to those events. Take your time, and allow yourself as much room as you need for your memories. Do this now,

M.'s memory trigger: A collection of music from her high-school years

taking as much time, as you need, returning to the text only when you're ready.

3. Now add other important events and memories you may have overlooked on the first go-around. Read and re-read the **Questions About Key Events** (page 146). Capture the key words of any other key events you remember, together with their associated memories. Return to the text when you are ready. Again, take all the time you need.

4. Welcome back. Now review all your memories of key events from the vantage point of others close to you. Ask yourself which of these events might have been important to your loved ones as well, from their perspective. Consider why these events might have been important to them, and how their feelings and behavior might have affected you?

Identifying Your Key Events at an Important Place

Welcome back. Now let's use as a trigger the memories you have already triggered using **Important Places in Your Life** (page 138). Find those memories and choose one place you would like to explore further. As you slowly review your memories of that place, ask yourself the questions that follow, capturing any new memories you get. Do this now.

At This Place:

1. Did a parent, close family member or friend die here? (What are your memories? Capture them.)

2. Was a parent or anyone close to you involved in a divorce? (What are your memories? Capture them.)

3. Was there was a reconciliation or separation?

4. Did you, or anyone close to you, suffer a serious illness or injury?

5. Were there serious arguments in your family?

6. Did you, or anyone close to you, experience outstanding personal achievements?

7. Did a family member leave or return home (because of school, a job, a marriage, military service, a divorce, etc.)

8. Did you move to a new home?

9. Did you, or anyone close to you, experience an outstanding financial success?

10. Or have alcohol, drug, or emotional problems?

11. Did you, or anyone close to you, marry?

12. Was there trouble with friends or neighbors?

13. Were there major changes for anyone at work (getting a promotion, losing a job, etc.)

14. Did anyone important to you retire or stop working for some reason?

15. Were there major changes in your family's living conditions?

16. Did you have an experience of any kind that you now understand affected you very deeply?

Using Your Memories in the Here-and-Now

Activities for you to do, and to do with friends and family

1. When you have an opportunity, share your memories of key events with someone close to you. Then ask them what they consider as the key events in *your* life (they may have a different idea than you) and about the key points in *their* lives.

2. Ask questions of others who may have experienced your key events in a different way than you did. The question might be: "When we moved to _____

_____

_____

_____

_____

_____

About this memory:
Reunions, visits to old
friends and to the
important *places* of one's
life–at whatever age–can
be among the most
powerful of all triggers,
and a powerful bonding
agent when experienced
with a partner or another
family member. This
memory was tape-
recorded after a visit to
the grave of my wife's
father, when she and I
talked from a place of
warmth and deep feelings
about what we had
experienced. Later we
would transcribe and
elaborate on our word
processors "for the
record" about what we
had experienced. Her
memory is important to
me because of what it
told me about my wife's
inner life. What a blessing
to relationships that must
deal with the legacy ▶ p. 151

(your key event, not necessarily theirs), what was
that like for you?" Their answers may trigger other
memories as well as help you to understand each
other better.

3. For a birthday or anniversary, stage a "This is Your
    Life" presentation for a friend or family member and
    recreate that person's life history through significant
    mementos, events and people.

"Your Uncle Frank Died"

"On this trip back to Pittsburgh, I got in touch with
Nancy, who had been my very, very best little friend,
and lived across the street from me from the very earliest
years. She and her husband picked us up and at some
point I told them that I wanted to see Grandpa's house on
Northumberland Street. It was the house where my father
had died when I was eight years old.

"When I saw the house, I suddenly had this compelling
need to be inside. First I went to the back door, which was
where the kitchen was, and peeked in the windows, and I
saw the kitchen, which had been modernized. This was a
house I hadn't been in for more than 50 years!

"Then I just had to go inside. Fortunately Nancy knew the
people who lived in the house, so when a housekeeper
came to the door she was frightened at first, but we were
able to make contact. I said, 'I lived here as a child. May I
please come in?' The housekeeper thought she would need
to get permission from the owner, but she wasn't able to
reach him, so she let us in. And Bob and I went through
the house slowly, room by room. Just the two of us.

"I was flooded with memories, and not all were painful.
Of sitting on the steps during my Aunt Mim's and Uncle
John's wedding. And sitting on the steps again with our
old family doctor. I must have been maybe four years old
at the time. And sitting on my father's lap at the piano.

"And then we went upstairs. I remembered exactly the room where I had been so ill at the same time that my father was down the hall dying of pneumonia. At that time there was no cure for it; people simply perished.

"So I was in my room with a very, very high fever and an ear infection, and he was down the hall in my parents' room ... I remember that I kept asking, Where's my father? Where's my father? Where's Daddy? Where's Daddy? And I was told that I couldn't see him, that I would see him when I got better and when he got better.

"Well, I got better and he was already dead and had been buried. Nobody had told me that my father had died.

"At some point I remember my Uncle Paul came into my room–I can remember exactly where he was standing at the foot of the bed. He said, 'Your Uncle Frank died.'

"And I remember my shock and saying, 'I don't have an Uncle Frank. My father is Frank and I have a brother Frank. I don't have an Uncle Frank.' But I knew. I knew. And you know, I don't remember ever, ever crying. It was like all I could do was just mobilize myself not to be too sad and scared, somehow to figure out how to take care of myself.

"I can't remember when my mother first acknowledged to me or had a conversation with me about his death. She was totally devastated by his death herself. She was a very young woman, maybe 29, with two very small children, and I think she simply didn't know what to do.

"As an adult I can understand, but as a child I felt like I had to take care of her, and my little brother, and myself. My whole world had fallen apart. My father literally disappeared.

"And then Nancy and Milton drove us to the cemetery where my father was buried. And I had long, long prepared for this visit to him. And Bob and I stood at the grave and I talked to my father as if he were there, and he

of old hurts and betrayals, many of them unavoidable but needing to be re-examined and updated with the insights of a wiser adult.

did come alive for me that day. I told him about my life, and how much I missed him during my whole life, and how I wanted him to know who I was.

"It was the most deeply moving and important visit I had ever paid. For so many years as a child, though my mind knew he was dead, at a deeper level I didn't accept it. My fantasies kept him alive; he was in the West somewhere, maybe he'd come back one day. (And I went West too, in my 30s.) This was a small child's inability to integrate such a sudden disappearance without adequate space to be sad, scared, and to grieve."

What Do *You* Remember?

Capture in the wide margins or in your notepad any memories you get as you answer these questions. Consider sharing your answers and your memories with friends and family, and asking about similar experiences in their lives.

1. When you were young, did anyone die who was important to you? What are your memories of that death? How did you learn about the death? How old were you? What were your feelings? Did you go to the funeral? Who was there?

2. As a small child, what was your understanding of the life-process—of death as part of the life process? Was anyone in your family open with you about death and what it meant? Were you able to talk with anyone about the deaths of important people in your life? What are your memories of these occasions?

3. Were you allowed or encouraged to cry at some moments? Was there someone there to hold you and allow you to have your sadness? Did any religious or spiritual beliefs grow out of that loss? Have you ever found that returning to painful memories–and sometimes sharing them with others–has left you feeling more positive and healed?

Important People in Your Life

In this chapter, you will:

- Create a list of important people in your life, triggering more memories as you do

- Learn more ways to use your memories creatively, for self-understanding, and to improve your relationships with others

- Read other's memories of important people in their lives that may trigger more memories of yours

I was 30, it was 1959, and I wanted to go to graduate school part-time to become a social worker. It seemed impossible. Go back to school with three small children to take care of? And I wanted to go part-time! It's hard to believe today, but this just didn't happen in those days— not in a single school of social work! Women who wanted careers were to stay home with their children until they were "older."

And then a new dean arrived. He forged the way for me, involving the faculty and even the university president; he wanted this experiment to work so that others could follow. And he got it to happen! He showed me how to achieve organizational change, which was what I wanted to learn about anyway. So Dean Nat Cohen became a major mentor of mine, and in later years my friend and colleague.

—JOAN, *65*

One Family's Important People

What's an important person? A family member, a teacher, a mentor, even someone not known to us personally. A person who taught us, served as a role model, supported us emotionally, or affected our lives, as a child or adult, in a significant way.

You may find that you would like to renew your acquaintance with those people who were so influential in your life. It might be revealing to ask them, at the appropriate time, to tell you who *their* major influences were, and why they were important to them. (In no special order.)

Father's
Earle Combs
Joe DiMaggio
Davie Kerr
Uncle Tom
Uncle George
Uncle Herman
Our Janitor
Billy Egan
Robert Montgomery
Kermit Rolland
C.F. MacIntyre
John H.H. Lyon
Susanne K. Langer
Milton Wayne
Jack Gibb
Dick Olney
Jack Abbott
Ruby Braff
Alec Wilder
My Wife

Arthur Schnitzler
E.B. White
Woody Allen
Jean Renoir
Grandpa
My Parents
My Children

Mother's
My husband
Father
Mother
Brother Frank
Grandpa
Sister Marj
Brother George
Grandmother
My Children
My Grandchildren
Erv Polster
"Doc" Churchill

Vladimir Horowitz
Nat Cohen
Dick Olney
Rae Weil
Arthur Rubinstein
Emily
JFK
Eleanor Roosevelt
Martin Luther King
Freud
Paulo Friere
Aunt Mim
Helen Palmer

Daughter's
Scott Kenny
Mrs. Bird
Mr. Michaelian
Lauren Yagle
John Kenny
My Father

My Mother
My Brother
My Sister
Mr. Spalding
Jeddo Patterson
Martin Ron
Ken Morse

Daughter's
Mrs. Kirk
Senor Carizo
Eva
Nadia Comaniche
Adam Brown
Maria Gray
Sofia Tawachi
Professor Yaeckle
Judge Fern Smith
Jennifer Symes
My Sister
Leslie Blank

Here's an exercise to help you trigger more memories about the important people in your life. They may be family members, teachers, mentors, even someone we did not know personally. They may have served us as role models, supported us emotionally, or affected our lives in a significant way. First I'll ask you to create a master list of those people, similar to the list of one family's important people on the opposite page.

It is those we live with and love and should know who elude us.

—THE FATHER
in Norman Maclean's
memoir,
A River Runs Through It.

Creating a Master List of Important People

1. For this exercise, you'll need several sheets of your 8-1/2 by 11 paper. As you did with your list of Places, divide the pages into two vertical columns, labelling the left-hand column "Important People" and the right-hand column "Memories." Do this now, after taking some time to liberate your physical and mental space from any distractions, and perhaps breathing deeply to focus your energy. ✋

2. In the left-hand column, list all the important people in your life until you think of no more. Don't try to rank them in order of importance; simply capture these names as they appear in your mind. As you remember each person, in the right-hand column, write the key words of any memories you are associating to that person. Take plenty of time to do this. You'll have an opportunity to review and add to this list later. When you're ready, return to the text. ✋

3. Welcome back. You may wish to stop for awhile before beginning the next part of this exercise. When you're ready, move on to the next step, where you'll use your memories of places to trigger more memories and perhaps names of more people.

A.'s memory trigger: Hearing old music or radio programs (her own or her parents')

Important People at the Places of Your Life

1. For this part of the exercise, use the same 8-1/2 by 11 sheets as before. Have handy your list of addresses where you've lived and the memories they have triggered. Also have handy all the other memories you have triggered so far. Please do this and return. ✋

2. As you review all the memories you have triggered so far, mark those that contain memories of a specific person: a parent, relative, friend, teacher, boss, colleague, hero or heroine. As you mark these names, be aware of any new or elaborated memories you are having about those people. Be aware also of any associations you are having to other people. Capture your names and the key words of your memories on your 8-1/2 by 11 sheets. Do this now, taking your time, and return to the text when you're ready. ✋

Questions About Important People

Now, as you consider one of your important places, find a name of one person that you feel attracted to. Keep that person in mind as you look at the following questions. It can be helpful to close your eyes after reading each set of questions, opening them only to capture your memories.

- When not with you, where was that person? Had you visited where she or he lived or worked? Or lived? Where was it? What did it look like? What happened there?

- Do you remember any furnishings or other contents you saw? Some things you particularly liked may be there. What were they? Were any family or friends likely to be there? Did you hear any special sounds here? Are you having any memories or feelings?

- If you visited a place with that special person, imagine that visit. What was it like? Imagine yourself inside the place. Did it have a distinctive odor? Walk through the rooms, taking your time as you go. Who was there with you?

- Continue to identify important people in as many place lists as you wish, adding to or expanding your memories each time.

Using Your Memories in the Here-and-Now

Activities for yourself, and to do with friends and family

1. Do you have photographs or other mementos of any of these important people? If you do, find them and see if you can trigger any more memories.

2. Share the names and photographs of your important people with someone you care for—chances are that some names will be unfamiliar to them. Volunteer to answer questions. Consider tape-recording your replies. You may want to transcribe them for a permanent journal or memoirs that can be shared with others.

3. Try to arrange a meeting—through a telephone call or letter—with some of your important people. Share your memories with them, and ask them how they responded to you.

B.'s memory trigger: Sharing stories about an important person with his loved ones (This is "Honorary Uncle Tom," p. 158)

About this memory:
Triggered by my created list of important people, these memories of my "Uncle Tom" are among my sweetest and most vivid. How *accurate* is it in its details? Was he who I thought he was? Did it actually happen this way? Did he feel as strongly about me? I can't say, and no one is around to answer these questions. And does it really matter, since this a memory that nourished me during childhood and one that I would not want to forget.

My Honorary Uncle Tom

Heroes? There would be movie stars (Fred Astaire, Robert Montgomery, and several blonde actresses); singers like Buddy Clark; bandleaders like Hal Kemp; and athletes like Joe DiMaggio, Earl Combs, Sid Luckman, and Cliff Montgomery. Some of my important people would be teachers, mentors, and people I would never meet, but who would teach me how to understand and get along in my world: C.F. McIntyre, Milton Wayne, Jack Abbott, Jack Gibb, Alec Wilder, Ruby Braff, Dick Olney. Mostly, my wife. Some captured my imagination for reasons I did not understand at the time. As a child, though, I was impressed by people in my parents' circle who seemed different from them and different from my expectations. Like my Uncle Tom.

"Uncle" Tom was an honorary uncle, a special friend of my parents. He was aggressive, hot-tempered (but not with me), unpredictable, and very handsome; he owned a garage or garages in midtown Manhattan.

In the thirties, we often vacationed with the Thomases. I liked the way he drove his Buick fast, at 35 miles an hour, challenging other cars when his son and I, screaming at the other cars, would urge him to.

Once, when all six of us–two sets of parents, two pre-teen boys–were on a trip to Asbury Park, I caught my thumb in the rear door getting out of his car. Somehow he and not my father or mother took me somewhere in the hotel, soaked my thumb in ice water and generally cared for me. I was bawling. Having Tom take care of me was something I remembered often. Why him? Why not my father?

Several years later, at my Bar Mitzvah party, congratulations were being offered from the stage, and Uncle Tom, having had a little much of the Manischevitz, surprised me–and everyone else in the room–by announcing to one and all that my mother, and not his wife, was the woman he had always loved and hoped to marry.

Now this was interesting, much more so than getting a whole bunch of fountain pens! I never knew how my father and Uncle Tom, who were very old friends, handled the situation, but my mother and "Aunt" Claire, who knew each other in high school, did not see each other as often after that, or so it seemed to me.

What Do *You* Remember?

Capture any memories you get as you answer these questions. Consider sharing your answers and your memories with friends and family, and asking them about similar experiences in their lives. Reflect carefully on each question before moving on.

1. In the wide margins, create a list of your favorite relatives, "honorary" aunts and uncles included. As you do, capture any memories that come up about the times you spent with them.

2. Think about your different relationships you had with each of those special people. And what you remember about their families. What did they mean to you? Capture any memories that are being triggered.

3. Did you parents know how important they were to you? What do you remember about how your parents felt about them.

Using Your Memories in the Here-and-Now

Activities for yourself, and to do with friends and family

1. Share your names of important people with someone you care for—chances are that some names will be unfamiliar to them. Volunteer to answer

_____

_____

_____

_____

_____

questions. Consider tape-recording your replies. You may want to transcribe them for a permanent journal or memoirs that can be shared with others.

2. Encourage those you share with to share their memories with you.

3. Try to arrange a meeting with some of the important people in your life. Tell them what you are remembering about them and ask them to share some memories with you.

About this memory:
Is there a family on the face of the planet without secrets? Perhaps "secret" is not the exactly right word, since something is likely to be known, but never quite enough. So the story is closed down, at least partially, by those who know the details; over time, children and grandchildren may learn more of the story, if they are interested. But never quite enough to remove the mystery from the drama.

Family Secrets

Looking through an old family photo album I remember my Uncle Herman, my mother's kid brother. He was probably about 15 years older than me but still a boy himself when I spent most of my time with him. Sullen and rebellious-looking in the few photographs I have of him. Always regarded as the family outcast, and always my favorite. At some point, Herman sort of disappeared from the family. I never kept track of family goings-on, but in retrospect I realize that we didn't see Herman very much.

The next-to-last time I see Herman I'm about 13, while my parents and my grandfather are visiting my maternal grandmother at a hospital. My mother is carrying a bouquet of flowers. As we enter the hospital corridor, on the way to my grandmother's room, my mother goes first, me somewhere behind, and I see my mother suddenly whirl around, come back toward me, her face contorted and angry, the flowers hanging limp at her side. "She's dead."

And then confusion and my mother focusses on the flowers, needing to get rid of them as quickly as possible. She looks for a waste basket, and flings the flowers into it, saying something about her mother not needing them now.

A few minutes later, we're all sitting in the back seat of the car. Someone talks about my grandfather moving in with us now, when suddenly Herman's face appears in the car window. (Had he been in the hospital before we arrived, perhaps even in his mother's room?) And then an explosive exchange between my grandfather and his son, at an intensity I had never heard. Herman–his life style, his work failures, his drinking, his favored son-ness–was being blamed for his mother's death. Herman was being disowned by his father.

Slowly, much later, I learn more. Herman held small jobs, drank too much, lived in a shabby rooming house, where he had an affair with the proprietor's daughter, who became pregnant, and he was "forced" to marry her. She was "beneath" our family both in appearance and in social station, and while Herman might, under other circumstances, be welcome in our home, his wife certainly was not.

I see Herman for the last time in my early 20s, soon after getting out of the Army, in my folks' apartment, waiting for them to return, and sitting around with some Army buddies. Herman had come to borrow money, and his wife was waiting downstairs in the lobby. He obviously adored me, and my friends (and I) were impressed with his conversation, his personality, and I suppose his glamour. My folks didn't show up, he left, I didn't ask to meet his wife, and didn't get his address.

Things went steadily worse for him and he ended up doing sanitation work in Hartford, and died in a "charity home" somewhere.

I came to be ashamed of my parents, over the way they treated their brothers and sisters. And I was ashamed for myself too, for I had obediently respected their wishes to isolate Herman from his family, and I might have made his life happier if I had gone to see him. And the worst thing was that we never talked about it, and now they're gone.

What Do *You* Remember?

Capture any memories you get as you answer these questions. Consider sharing your answers and your memories with friends and family, and asking them about similar experiences in their lives. Reflect carefully on each question before moving on.

1. Was your family private and secretive? If they were, how did you know they were? Was there a big secret in the family? How did you feel about it? Did you feel that you heard only part of the story? What questions would you have asked, if you could have?

2. When you learned a secret as a child, did you keep it to yourself or share it with someone? How old were you when you learned the secret? How did it happen exactly?

3. If you shared a secret, who did you tell? How did you feel about telling? And how was the secret received by whomever you told?

4. After childhood, did you learn of other secrets in your family? How did you find out? How did you feel when you found out?

5. Do you remember secrets you had–about yourself or others–that you never shared with anyone. What were they, and how do you feel about this secrecy now?

My Foster Mother's Place

"When I was an infant in Montreal, I was sent to live a foster home, where I stayed until I was six or so. There usually weren't any children to play with. So my foster mother—I called her Aunt Beth—did things to keep me entertained.

"She liked to bake. She would put me on a high kitchen stool at the counter and put stuff in the bowl and stir it up, and while she was doing that she would say poetry to me.

"She would say a line, and I would say it. And she would say two lines and I would say two lines. And then after awhile I learned poetry. I used to know all of Hiawatha, 'By the shores of Gitche Gumee,' all that stuff. You know I can still recite it!

"It wasn't like learning. It never felt 'hard,' like somebody sat me down and taught me poetry. It was just about being together, and hearing what she had to share. So there was poetry in the kitchen along with everything else.

"Like the wonderful sweet kitchen smells of bread baking in the oven, the gingerbread, and lemon icing, because that was one of my favorite things, hot gingerbread!

"Right after Thanksgiving she would bake shortbread cookies—they were mostly butter!—and put them in tins with wax paper between the layers of cookies to separate them.

"They looked nice too, so they became Christmas gifts in their red tins. It was a lovely thing, and so social, having people into your home, and sharing your home with them, bringing gifts, being very much a part of the family. When you'd go to somebody's house, you'd always take something.

"Bear in mind that I'm in Canada, in the only black family for miles around. But even when I was a little girl, I could

About this memory:
Sometimes, when the occasion seems right, I interview my friends about their childhoods, sometimes using a tape recorder. This time, since three of us were in the kitchen preparing to eat, I asked questions about food: What was your favorite food? How did they butter corn in your family? (Show me.) How did you go after an ice cream cone—from the top? Sides? Did you lick it or bite into it? (Show me.) When we're listening to my music, I might ask about theirs: Whose music did you listen to in high school? Who were your favorite performers? Who did you listen with?

The conversation soon moves on to other things, sometimes quite serious ones, and we all feel better about one another, as we did here.

recite from memory, verse after verse, poem after poem, black dialect poetry I learned from my foster mother. Like Paul Laurence Dunbar—'little brown baby with sparkling eyes.' I had forgotten that until I went to a poetry reading when I was an undergraduate at Berkeley. And I found I could recite along with this woman reading the poetry and all these deep memories returned.

"My memories of my foster mother are all triggered by food, all in the kitchen. Sitting up there on the stool. Dangling my legs when she's talking. Maybe she'd let me pour the sugar. Sometimes she'd let me lick the bowls.

"She found ways to keep a little girl quite happy. *(Speaking in a childish hush)* I would set the table, clean the silver, and wash it in the soap, and rinse it. I have no memory of that being work! She'd say, isn't that beautiful?

"Now I'm remembering playing outside in the yard with a white boy about my own age, when he called me a nigger and my foster mother heard him.

"She was a very forceful woman. She marched him over to his house and told his parents, "I've brought your son back. He does not know how to act.' And she was finished with him. I never played with that boy again, ever.

"She saved my life. But my foster father was wonderful too. When he came home from work, he was just mine until bedtime. And he loved it. He was in his 60s and had never had any children. Here was this little girl who was delightful and playful and cute. He used to let me ride on the handle bars of his bicycle. Now that I think about it, I realize how he must have exerted himself. He had emphysema, and the things he did with me must have been hard for him. But I didn't know that then.

"I would not have been able to survive what was to come without them. Because they taught me I was just fine."

What Do *You* Remember?

1. If you spent any time as a young child living (or being with someone: a relative, maid, teacher, mentor, etc.) outside of your own family or origin, how did that experience affect you and your sense of yourself?

2. What effect did those relationships have on the way you developed, learned, played, and grew into adulthood?

3. Who were the other important influences in your life besides your parents? Who might have "saved your life" or changed the direction of your life in some significant way? How long were they in this role? How did they find you, or how did you find them?

Organizing Your Memories

In this chapter, you will:

- Learn several ways of organizing your memories—by time period, by key event, by important people, and by places.

- Learn the various forms that your memory collection can take.

The task is to see and hear and learn and understand; and write when there is something that you know; and not before; and not too damned much after. Let those who want to save the world if you can get to see it clear and as a whole.

—ERNEST
HEMINGWAY

On the following page: how members of one family organized their different memory albums, with their memories divided by key events in their lives, and then in chronological order within those time periods.

One Family's Way of Organizing Memories in Their Memory Albums

Father, 69
My mother
Beginning elementary school
Graduating from high school
Induction into Army
Discharge from Army
Divorce
Arrival in California
Divorce
Meeting Constance and Jack
Meeting Joan
The Firestorm

His Wife, 62
Baby brother born
Father dies suddenly (2 years later)
Mother's remarriage
Acquisition of two siblings
Being sent to girl's private school
First year in college
Encampment for Citizenship
Getting married
Becoming a mother
Going to graduate school,
   developing a career
Moving to Washington, DC
   and job at UPO
Getting doctorate
Self-Acceptance Training
Marrying Bob
Becoming a grandparent

Eldest Daughter, 33
Moving to California
Children's ballet
Accident, quitting ballet
Parents' divorce
Mom going to Panama
Going to Tam High
Meeting John
Marriage
Scott's birth
Moving to the country

Youngest Daughter, 27
Experience in Day Care
Elementary school bussing
Moving to Panama
High school
Return to the U.S.
First Love
Going to the University
Law school in Boston
Externing in San Francisco
David

Son, 35
Sickness as a kid
Moving to California
Parents' divorce
First job in film industry
Breakup with K.
Engagement to Shelley

So where are you? Very likely you've done all or some of the exercises. You've found that some exercises have been more productive than others, not necessarily because of the number of memories you have triggered, but in the importance and meaning of certain memories, and how several memories have interacted with others to provide new meanings, and because of what happened when you shared your memories with others.

You've captured your key words in the book margins, or in a notepad, loose-leaf binder, or in a word processor or tape recorder, or in some other way that felt comfortable to you.

And now I encourage you to organize your captured memories, for two reasons.

- First, you will have a more permanent and interesting record than you now have—much like a family photograph album or slide collection that can be shared by many others through the generations.

- Second, as you organize and rearrange your memories into a different order and format, you will both trigger new memories and also trigger details and elaborations about memories you have already triggered.

This chapter suggests some patterns to begin with. Again, there's no right way. You might wish to abandon your first choice and try another. Choose the one that is most appealing and most practical for you:

Chronological Order

Arrange your memories in chronological order, in broad time periods. If you're under 40, you might prefer a five-year organization; if over forty, a ten-year organization. Simply review all the key words and elaborations you have

They are passing, posthaste, posthaste, the gliding years.... The years are passing, my dear, and presently no one will know what you and I know.

VLADIMIR NABOKOV
Speak, Memory

P.'s memory trigger: Bob en route to New Guinea, 1944

triggered and place them into the correct time slot, as accurately as you can.

Key Events

Arrange your memories by key events—those events you realize have had the most impact on your life and which changed the direction of your life. All or most of these key events can be found in your responses to the exercise beginning on page 147.

Important People

Arrange them by important people in your life–family and non-family members–reviewing all the memories you have triggered so far and arranging them in this way.

Places

You can arrange your memories by the places you lived in (you already have a good start on doing this.)

Any Combination of the Above

For an example, see the exhibit on page 168. Remember to choose any method–including any that is not included here–that is pleasurable and practical for you.

The Form of Your Memory Collection

You also need to decide what form your collection of memories will take. Implementing some options will take a little more time and money than others.

- *Should it be a "memory album" or other document that could become part of your family legacy? (Over the years, you could also add important photographs, documents and mementos to your collection.)*

- *A type of journal or diary?*

- *A written memoir?*

• *A personal history on video tape?*

You might get a tripod, turn the camera on yourself, and tell the camera, over time, your memories and their meaning. You might speak into the camera while you're thinking of your grandchild–or a future grandchild–who may be more curious about your life than your own children.

You might volunteer to be interviewed by someone important to you–giving that person your organized memories and key words, and being available for any questions that might be asked.

• *Or a personal history on audio tape?*

If you choose audio, be certain you obtain high quality tape, and a sensitive microphone, preferably a lavaliere type that clips to a collar, blouse or tie. Never begin until you have tested the microphone, and consider replacing your batteries every time you begin another recording session. It's a good investment to protect the priceless information you will be collecting, which will never be as powerful if you have to re-record it at a later date. And be sure to label your audio and video tapes carefully, and perhaps make a duplicate copy in case yours should be lost or damaged.

• *You may also plan your memory organizing project as a cooperative family affair, completed with others in the family who may wish to add their own memories, writing, voices, and spoken comments to whatever you do.*

Whichever format you choose should be open-ended; as the years go on, you can add more pages, volumes, or tapes as you continue to trigger more memories and refine your collection.

Our lives are ceaselessly intertwined with the stories that we tell and hear told, those we dream or imagine or would like to tell, all of which are reworked in that story of our own lives that we narrate to ourselves in a....virtually unin-terrupted monologue. We recount and reassess the meaning of our past actions, and anticipate the outcome of our future projects....The narrative impulse is as old as our oldest literature.

—PETER BROOKS

D. & S.'s memory trigger: Bringing out souvenirs from their vacation trips

■ ■ ■

What gifts to leave your grandchildren and children! How many of us lose our parents and grandparents and wonder forever about important incidents in their lives we never asked about, and now will never be able to ask! Why did Dad leave the family? What exactly did happen in the War? What really happened to Cousin Mike? What did Grandpa do? We mean to ask and there never seems to be enough time, and then the opportunity is gone.

As there is no right way to trigger, there's no right way to assemble your memory collection. Do whatever is most comfortable and productive to you. And begin whenever you can.

FLYING A KITE ON A WINDY DAY

VISTING A RELATIVE OUT O

YOUR FIRST PET

EPILOGUE

SINGING SONGS AROUND A C

VING CROSS-COUNTRY WITH YOUR FAMILY

THE SOUND OF A FOGHORN

The Firestorm

Joan Cole and Bob Wendlinger

Memories can be an agent of self-restoration and self-healing. We learned this after the experience that destroyed our home and 3,000 others in the worst urban firestorm in modern history, when we used our memories (intentionally triggered and otherwise) to reconstitute our lives and recover from the loss of the precious personal possessions of a lifetime. The principal triggers were our continuing memories of the fire, and our terror, and our escape–how could we not recall them, and often? At the same time, however, we were also able to create memory maps and floor plans, similar to those you have already created, to help us recall and capture the precious possessions we had lost within that house.

While the large majority of those possessions had no history and were easily replaceable, lost forever were many meaningful and irreplaceable old objects–Joan's grandmother's antique lamps, her dad's pocket watch and chain, Bob's father's sales awards, photographs of ancestors, and others of ourselves and our children when we were all young. All of these were among the many things which held enormous meaning that the trauma of the fire had temporarily obliterated and that we could not afford to lose.

After the fire, some people said of our loss, hoping, we're sure, to console us: "Well, it's just things." What they could not have known was that certain of these things had become imbued with powerful personal meaning and with many generations of family history. And we knew that–if we were not to lose much more than a home–our legacies, our histories, simply had to be recovered in our psyches and retained in some way. The way for us was to go deeply within ourselves and remember as many of those things, memories, and meanings as we could–by image, by feel,

*And what you thought you came for
Is only a shell, a husk of meaning
From which the purpose breaks
   only when it is fulfilled
If at all. Either you had no purpose
Or the purpose is beyond the end
   you figured
And is altered in fulfillment.*

—T. S. ELIOT
Four Quartets

by texture, by sound. To remember what **was.** This was our way of soothing ourselves and providing continuity with the past in our personal lives.

So two years after the fire, we collaborated to trigger memories not only of the terrible event that destroyed our house and its contents, but to capture much of the meaning and life-history that were contained within some of those precious possessions.

Oakland, California, October 20, 1991. It's an extraordinarily hot Sunday morning, and we are scurrying about, preparing to have brunch for family and friends in celebration of the 85th birthday of Joan's mother. She is here from Cleveland, and, because of her difficulty in climbing the stairs in our house, staying with her companion at a hotel down the hill, a few minutes away. She will be here later. Meanwhile, Gloria, our helper, is cleaning up; Joan is cooking; Bob is sweeping the deck and bringing out the toys we store downstairs anticipating our grandchildren's visits. There's an excitement in the air about this event: 25 or 30 people, including many elders and children, are expected to arrive in about an hour. Much to do and for Joan especially, as always a special kind of joy in the preparing of a meal and a social event.

Pete (Joan's son), Ann and the little girls have arrived early from Sacramento, are across the street at the community swimming pool, after volunteering to stay out of our way so we can prepare for the party. Having them there for the weekend gives us both familiar feelings of well-being, a deep inner joy at being with them... A feeling that all is right with the world, full and warm.

Yet, on this day, Joan's feelings are mixed with a certain unease which grows more intense as the morning progresses. For her, actually nothing seems to be going well. It was as in a dream she had earlier that morning, where she is struggling to appear at a very important appointment, but doesn't know what to wear, at first can't find her car, and then finds the road blocked. Anxiety conquers her psyche in this dream, and the tension will only be relieved if she is able to make the appointment or wake up. She awakens, wondering what this dream means in the context of our life today.

We've all had such dreams and nightmares, of course. And this day **was** like the dream. First, there was the unprecedented heat on our hillside, mixed with extraordinarily high winds, the kind that Californians a call Santa Ana. At around 11 o'clock Bob is on the deck, returning from the garage, and a gust of wind sends a thick layer of leaves onto the deck, and into the luscious garden which Joan had just completed two months before. He thinks (as he tells Joan later), "Damn, Joan is going to ask me to sweep this up one more time before the guests arrive!"

And then another gust, and another. And almost immediately the sky turns dark, and the light turns to pale yellow, and after a flash of blackness the sun turns scarlet! The sun was bizarre in the black sky—grave. It was unlike anything we had ever seen before. As Joan walked onto the deck, her first thought was that this was it: the nuclear holocaust we all have reason to dread had happened. She felt as if it was the end of life as we had known it. That turned out to be true, but blessedly, not in such global terms. Indeed, it was the end of life as we had known and trusted it, with its continuity and its safety now in the past.

Pete, Ann and the girls appeared at the house. At pool-side, they had seen the fire coming from another direction and were entirely clear that we must all leave. Elizabeth, just 5 years old, was in terror. As her parents prepared to flee, collecting nothing but a few dry clothes (they were in their wet bathing suits), Joan sat on the floor with Elizabeth. She held her tight as her small body shook in terror.

Hannah, then just a year and a half, showed no visible signs of fear, and her parents held onto her as they gathered themselves to escape. They fled moments later, heeding us to follow quickly.

Though we had lived in this house for only a year and a half, it was the first home that we had purchased and furnished together. It was truly our place, marked by our collective aesthetic, and planned to meet our particular needs, and those of our children, grandchildren and many friends. Walls were lined with family photographs, pictures of special friends and events. Music filled every room, and it had, in this year and a half, become a sanctuary of beauty and quiet, as well as liveliness and community.

Two months before the fire we had hosted our dear friends Barbara and Russell's wedding on our patio (they were also to lose their house). Holidays were spent there with friends and family. The home we created together had nurtured our bodies and our souls. We loved it, not so much as a structure, but for the "feel" of it: the colors, shape and comfort which we cherished.

In the few minutes which we had to gather ourselves–no more that ten minutes, probably less–Joan did several rather prototypical things. Extrovert that she is, she makes several phone calls warning people not to come to the party. "There's a fire, stay away—don't come to this side of town." (In retrospect–how absurd!) She could well have used those five minutes to get our wedding pictures, her father's pocket watch and precious chain, and other very valuable and sentimentally important jewelry and other family treasures, now gone forever.

Joan no longer tortures herself about that impulse to make contact with people, to warn her children and a few friends (and the caterer!) of the danger on the hillside; it took some months for her to deeply appreciate that this choice was her way of staying in connection to dear ones.

She also (literally) screamed at Bob to get his computer
into the car, believing full well that had he lost his book
(this book) and his research he could have died of a
broken heart. So we fled, with the flames encircling our
house, coming down the hillside at a speed that defied the
capacity of the human eye and human consciousness to
embrace. Awesome! (Later, the flames were reported to be
moving at 300 feet a minute.) And, as we would see in a
few moments, flames were moving up the hill as well as
down, moving rapidly through the brush toward our
house. Large cinders began to cover the deck and the roof.
As this happens, Joan knows that her life will be forever
altered...that we will never again see this house or this
neighborhood again as we have known it.

Outside now, Bob sees our neighbor Robin leave his house
across the street, look up at the hill, go inside, come out
again. As we are packing the car, another neighbor, confused
and in shock, asks whether it might be time to hose down
our roofs. Joan commands him to flee, and he does a kind of
pirouette as he leaves.

Traffic snarls the road as we turn into the only major road
down from the hills. Joan's hand rests tightly over her
mouth. She's unable to speak or to think clearly. Looking
at our hill beginning to go up in flames is nearly
unbearable, but her eyes are riveted on the fire and the
surrounding darkness.

Bob, stoic and still in some denial, has left valuables that
were within easy reach as we left: perhaps making a kind
of offering to fate: "If I leave them, then we must be
allowed to return?" In the car, he excepts what he has been
denying all along—Where is the help?—but says aloud that
he is optimistic that fire trucks will soon be here to save
the day. None, however, are in sight at this point, even
though the hill now is ablaze. No fire or police siren or
helicopter loudspeaker is audible. So his optimism does
not last for long, but meanwhile it forces Joan's complete

knowledge of the reality. It is as if she has to speak the truth for both of us. We will never be back. It's gone. Halfway down the hill, Bob too gives up hope. Yes, the fire is out of control and no one is coming.

Hunched over the wheel of the car, Joan cries, "What are we supposed to be learning now?" This is the question that has directed our lives and our consciousness for more than two years, and may be the major question which we will spend the rest of our time on this earth exploring and trying to answer. This traumatic life-event would indeed forever alter our consciousness, triggering old memories and pain, and surprisingly (although we did not know this at the time), creating new meanings, insights and hope for the future. We could not have imagined then that our memories of this fire would have such a deep and positive importance in our lives.

Our response to the fire began with a feeling of power-lessness, and Joan's belief that she could control her life was forever altered. But meanwhile the healing had begun, and our power to control more and more aspects of our lives began to return (returning to work, rebuilding our home, refurnishing it, fighting for our integrity with a bank and an insurance company).

Returning to our rebuilt home 14 months after the fire, we continued to experience the inevitability of memories being triggered by certain events: a hot windy day similar to that day of the fire; our knowledge of another fire, nearby or hundreds of miles away, seen on television; our awareness of a hot breeze floating in an unusual direction; the siren of a fire chief's car; an accident on the highway.

Breath-stopping images have appeared uninvited as Bob drives down our hill, now filled with newly built homes: images of blackened redwood trees and earth covered with gray ash, spotted with burnt and misshapen piano frames, twisted metal files, an unrecognizable vase recovered in the ruins where our house had been, and the contorted remains of heavy kitchen and bathroom equipment, some fragments appearing like abstract sculpture. This image of destruction disappears, is replaced with tears, and Bob has yet another image of escaping down the hill with Joan into another life.

Fire memories return, along with mood-swings into the depths of feeling, when triggered by fire questions from casual acquaintances; by lost objects seen again in stores, reminding us of what was and will no longer be, and of course, by the lost photographs, which signified our unique identity and the continuity of our lives, seconds away from recovery and left behind in panic. This was true for Bob in particular. While both of us were able to quickly recover many of them with the help of our families and friends, Bob's were more difficult to obtain, and he is still seeking photographs of his father's parents and his mother's youngest brother—his Uncle Herman.

The Oakland Firestorm was similar to those life-defining losses of larger and smaller magnitude which inevitably occur during life—losses caused by fires, earthquakes, floods, war, violent crimes, debilitating illness, the death of loved ones, the need to flee one's native land. And oddly enough, as totally traumatic as the fire was, we feel somehow ahead of the game, knowing deeply some things about our strength, resilience and creativity that we might not have known if it had not occurred.

The memories of our life we were triggering helped us to recover the sense of continuity, permanence, and meaning that we thought we had lost with our precious photographs and other possessions. So, truth to tell, the fire brought some pleasant surprises. We are now living life minute by minute, day to day, with exquisite attention to the beauty of each moment, to each contact with loved ones, to each sunrise and sunset. Mozart sounds more pure than ever. Bach's simplicity signifies the simple (and complex) nature of sound and of life. We believe more than ever before that the lesson of life is in the living—and in the concentrated appreciation of each moment.

Back in our beloved home, we've made a few nice changes, like removing a wall that was obstructing a view, and moving the fireplace to a cozier corner. We are back on the same ground, ashes not long before, because it is where we chose to live, and we have faith that it will once again feel safe and serene, even while we accept our lack of control of this world, and realize deeply how unpredictable and uncontrollable this life can be. Joan has learned to arrange flowers the formal Ikebana way—with special attention given to balance, harmony, and form; Bob has finished this book. The unexpected fire and its memories presented us with both a crisis of the spirit and a magnificent opportunity for personal growth.

A "Remembered" Father: Unexpected Pleasures

When triggered memories begin to accumulate, they begin to interact with one another, with the result that they can communicate more complex and richer meanings. When this happens, seemingly disparate memories of places, people, and events suddenly make more sense; memories triggered months before suddenly trigger new feelings, new insights and new meanings. Has this happened to you?

Sometimes this synergism will happen without any effort on your part, as your triggered memories, now conscious, begin to interact inside of you. You can also help to make it happen, by organizing your scattered memories into categories. For example, I collected all my memories of my father into a single computer. So the file consisted of my memories, mostly newly triggered; a few facts I knew about him, and some things he had said in his letter of some thirty years ago (partially transferred at some point to the computer, although his original letter was lost in the fire.)

> In this remembrance, the facts I know about my father, mostly from that letter, are interspersed with my triggered memories, which appear in *italics*. In parentheses and enclosed in quotations ("I did not do too well") are my father's brief written comments about his life, also taken from his letter.

Organized this way and brought into my consciousness for the first time, these memories have helped to create a fresh–and more positive–sense of who my father was and how he might have felt about me. My remembered father became a quite different person from the one that child thought he knew. So long after he was gone, my memories have altered my understanding of him, my clarity about his life, and most important, how I feel about him now. Hooray for triggering and surprises!

My father was born in 1891 in Drohobych, then part of the Austro-Hungarian Empire, later part of Poland, Czechoslovakia and Austria, now a border city in Russia. He came to the Lower East Side of New York City at the age of four, probably with his mother, his father probably having arrived earlier to find work, as was the custom. He was the youngest in a family of four whose father, disabled from a mining accident in Galecia (with a lead plate in his head), eked out a small income by doing pressing jobs first on the Lower East Side, then in a small Bronx apartment.

When I was a child and Dad was in the house, which

(it seemed) was not very often, it's usually night-time. He's sitting at the dining room table, with his back to the kitchen, where I am, and he's not about to be interrupted. Sometimes he's counting very large stacks of currency. Or adding columns in a three-inch book-size ledger, and afterward copying one entire ledger into another! My mother explained later that the ledgers were not his, but turned in by his agents for auditing. But they were not neat enough for him, and he wanted to present them to his boss in as neat a condition as possible.

He graduated from P.S. 188 (between Avenue D and Lewis Street), and his first school was on Second Street between Avenues C and D. Then he transferred to P.S. 79 on First Street between First and Second Avenues. He did not attend high school, although he received a high school equivalency certificate in mid-life.

I was afraid of my father. One of my earliest dreams was of being beaten for eating his tomato! (My mother said he never touched me.) While horsing around in my bedroom with another boy, I remember splitting a post at the foot of my four-poster bed. Awaiting his return from work, I was terrified. And then my mother, perhaps because the other boy had stayed in the room with me and the episode needed to be treated lightly, treated it playfully, suggesting that I get a hacksaw and even off both posts at their roots before my father came home. When he came home, nothing happened. (Today, I would like to know whether he did not notice, or noticed and said nothing, or was told at the door to not notice, or... so many scenarios! Of course, I will never know whether I had cause to be afraid of him.)

He worked from the age of thirteen ("odd jobs"), having become the main support of his parents and his older sisters. At fifteen he was an office boy in a buying office specializing in women's hats. At seventeen he sold ostrich

feathers on commission to the millinery trade ("I did not
do too well.")

> *One time, when I was in high school, the three of us
> were having dinner. I was detailing some exploit or
> another to my parents when my mother suddenly told
> me that she hoped I would do better in the world than
> my father had—I heard "better" to mean "make more
> money." I looked quickly at him and saw no change in
> his expression. I wanted an opportunity to defend him,
> and to defend myself. But I said nothing, and was
> ashamed of myself. And I hated her as I never had
> before.*

In 1914, when he was 23, he was exempted from Army
service during World War I because of his family
obligations. ("It is my opinion that I was exempted
because I was born in Austria.")

> *As I watch someone fearfully pulling out a lamp plug
> by its wire, afraid to touch the plug itself, I feel proud,
> and think of Dad. I'm a pre-teen, I guess, and he's
> sitting close to me, teaching me to use a circuit board
> and a large dry cell, while I learn not to be afraid of
> electricity.*

He sold buckram frames to millinery houses, ("did well"),
and four years later went into business for himself, at
125th Street and Madison Avenue, with borrowed money.
("I had not been able to save any money as I was
practically the support of my family.") ("Did quite well.")

> *I watch in fascination as he pours ketchup on his
> scrambled eggs. (So do I, today.) I see him turning the
> salt shaker upside-down, over whatever he was eating
> the time, letting it pour until my mother said,
> "Enough!" or something like that. I see him at the
> kitchen table, chewing a mouthful of food far too long,
> and I remember the lovely A.W., a date in my early
> 20s, at a fashionable East Side restaurant, her eyes*

_____

_____

_____

_____

_____

_____

_____

_____

_____

_____

_____

_____

_____

_____

_____

focussed on my face, watching a similar sight, and crying: "Swallow!"

He married my mother in 1921, when he was 30 and she was 24. They moved briefly to the Grand Concourse and then to Washington Heights, in Manhattan. Two years later, he moved his factory to the then-millinery center on West 36th, and began a small mail order business. In his late 30s, the bottom dropped out of his business, as the style in women's hats changed, his mother and father died within months of each other, and he ran out of capital and went out of business in 1927. ("Had auctioneer sell everything we had, paid all of our debts [fools that we were] and that was the end of the millinery business for me.") This was just before the Great Depression.

My mother tells a story about my father: Their courtship lasted six years, partly because *her* father was not certain that he could support her. Also, he was 24 when they met and she was only eighteen, just out of high school and working. She said she fell in love with him when he came to her office as a salesman, and she noticed that his spats were soiled!

I remember him as quite a fancy dresser, with a closet full of suits, all beautifully pressed. As styles changed, and lapels grew narrower, he would send his suits off to have the lapels altered.

A distant relative found him a job selling insurance at Metropolitan Life, the largest insurance company in New York. He quickly rose to a position of assistant manager, and then was blocked from further advancement (he believed) by his lack of formal education, by his sponsor being out of favor with senior management, and by his being Jewish.

I'm at my desk in my bedroom, using an upright Underwood typewriter that my father had bought for me, typing copy for my school newspaper on a large stencil using a blue ribbon that comes off on my fingers. The typewriter was a wonderful present but the dealer overcharged me five dollars when I picked it up, and Dad got very angry, at the dealer and at me. He decides he will straighten it out himself rather than have me return to the shop.

He worked 30 years for the Met, recognizing early on that he would never be promoted, unhappy most of the time, and apparently lacking the time or energy to try another career, as my mother had urged. Most of those in his circle of old friends were doctors or lawyers, owned small businesses or (like his brother-in-law) were successful salesmen. My mother had good taste and was an excellent money manager, and their life style (except for vacations) seemed very much the equal of his other friends.

I see him, after picking up his suits back from the cleaners, at an ironing board in the living room. He would pin his trouser creases into place, re-press his trousers, and then reblock them, using a heavy eighteen-inch long presser's block that had been his father's, and slamming the block down so hard on the crease that the thump would be heard throughout the house! I wonder now: was this his tribute to, or his learning from, his father, who pressed clothes for a living, confined to his apartment with his head injury?

In his 40s, Dad developed tuberculosis, then had a heart attack in his 50s, but he recovered and continued to work until he was 62 and the winters in New York were getting to him (they were living on Riverside Drive, near Columbia). My mother encouraged him to retire to Miami Beach, where he lived seemingly at peace until he died twenty years later.

I remember, as a child and young adult, being ashamed when Dad snorted. He would pull in a tremendous amount of air through his nose, making a terrible sound, and I suppose clearing his sinus passages. Since I had been taught (by example) that our family was not supposed to call attention to itself, I'm sure that this habit displeased my mother also.

(In recent years, I have begun to snort also, but mostly privately. When I must snort in my wife's presence, I am surprised when she does not seem to take notice. The question is, am I doing it because I have the same afflictions as my father? Or am I doing it as some kind of unconscious tribute to him, as when I chew my food interminably before swallowing, as he did? Who knows?)

I'm standing alongside his death-bed, having come to say goodbye. At home in Miami Beach, afraid of going to the hospital, he seemed not resigned but angry. With me? With dying? With what? I couldn't tell. Even now we could not talk to one another. He did direct me to take care of my mother, and I did.

I'm still discovering my father (and myself). Although he's been dead for 20 years now, and unavailable for my unanswered questions, memories continue to arise, and more mysteries. How happy were my parents? What did it mean when he would skip breakfast at home and instead go to Bickford's? (He would say: "They make oatmeal a special way there.") Was he a good businessman or not? And whether he was or not, why didn't he teach me how to get along in business? Was he interested in me? Did he really like me? Did he ever smile at me?

Some questions about my father will forever go un-answered, since no one is around who can answer them. Yet, as I trigger memories of events and spaces that we shared, look again at photographs of him, hold those things of his that remain, re-read the details of his important letter to me, ask others about him, and over time place the known and the unknown parts of his life together, he feels more real to me, more complex, more vulnerable, and more human. I enjoy (indeed, find delight in) this complexity and these discoveries of who he was and might have been.

Most important, as I place the known and the unknown parts of his life together, not only in my writing but in my consciousness, I enjoy my newly found empathy for his life, and the recognition of my love and compassion for him—very little of which I could feel during his lifetime.

So while I regret deeply what I never knew about him, and what we never created together, knowing him more fully opens many windows to knowing myself.

Knowing him better also enlivens and enriches my own life and my connections to those close to me, including my own children (the catalyst of this triggering project many years ago).

FLYING A KITE ON A WINDY DAY

VISTING A RELATIVE OUT O

YOUR FIRST PET

APPENDIX

SINGING SONGS AROUND A C

VING CROSS-COUNTRY WITH YOUR FAMILY

THE SOUND OF A FOGHORN

Other Sources of Memory Triggers

By now you're probably more aware than ever of memories being triggered spontaneously by elements in your environment: scents, sounds, places, and so forth. Sometimes, simply as fun, you may want to track down particular movies, radio programs, and books that you know or suspect can trigger still more memories. If you do, this source list of memory triggers can help.

Old Movies

Critics' Choice Video, 800 Morse Avenue, Elk Grove Village, IL 60007 1-800-544-9852.

> Cartoons and TV shows from the 30s to 70s, on video tapes. Our Gang, Three Stooges, Bugs Bunny, "cliffhanger" serials, Dick Tracy, I Love Lucy, The Honeymooners, Nat Cole, Ernie Kovacs, Burns & Allen, Jack Benny, documentaries, etc.

Warner & Sony Sound Exchange. Your Greatest Year Videos. 45 N Industry Ct., Deer Park, NY 11729.

> Archival newsreel footage from 1929-1967.

Vintage Radio Programs

Radio Yesteryear and Video Yesteryear, Box C, Sandy Hook, Conn. 06482. 1-800-243-0987.

> Vintage radio and TV broadcasts from the 30s, 40s, and 50s on audio cassettes, video cassettes, and LPs.

Terrace, Vincent. *Radio's Golden Years:* The Encyclopedia of Radio Programs 1930-1960

Television from the 50s and 60s

Time-Life Video, 1450 E. Parham Road, Richmond, Va. 23280.

> Historic documentaries (World War II, lives of famous people, etc.) as well as old feature films and radio programs on video cassettes and audio tapes.

Brooks, Tim and Earl Marsh. *The Complete Directory to Prime Time Network TV Shows 1946-present.* Ballantine Books, 1981.

Original Master Recordings

Time-Life Music, 1450 E. Parham Road, Richmond, Va. 23280.

Collections of country music, rhythm and blues, rock and roll, big band swing, "Your Hit Parade," etc., by the original artists.

• Surveys

Billboard's Pop Memories (1920-1959). (6 CDs). Rhino Records.

Nipper's Greatest Hits (1901-1978) (11 CDs) RCA Records.

• By Decade

Those Wonderful Years: Swing Time (1930-1940) RCA/Essex Records.

Themes of the Big Bands (1931-46) Intersound

Woodstock 25th Anniversary Collection: Three Days of Peace and Music. (2 CDs) Atlantic.

60s Rock Classics. (2 CDs) Rhino Records Special Edition.

Billboard's Top Rock and Roll Hits (1950-1972) (22 CDs) Rhino Records.

The Best of Chess Rhythm and Blues. (2 CDs) Chess Records.

• Holiday Music

Greatest Christmas Hits (1935-1983). (2 CDs) Rhino Records.

Music Directories

Whitburn, Joel. Pop Memories 1890-1954: The History of American Popular Music.

_____. *The Billboard Book of Top 40 Hits:* 1956-on.

_____. *Top Country and Western Records:* 1944-1987.

> Available in some bookstores and from Record Research Inc., P.O. Box 200, Menomonee Falls, WI 53042.

Cartoon Music

"The Carl Stallings Project: Music from Warner Bros. Cartoons 1936-1958"

> A CD of soundtracks by film composer Carl Stallings for Bugs Bunny and other cartoons.

Sheet Music

Readers Digest. *Remembering Yesterday's Hits: A Readers Digest* Songbook

_____. *Parade of Popular Hits: A Readers Digest* Songbook

Media Museums

Museum of Television and Radio, 25 West 52nd Street, New York, N.Y. 10019. 212-621-6600.

> Probably the world's largest collection of radio and television broadcasts, and open to the public. The radio collection begins in 1920; the television collection in 1939.

An Early Life Questionnaire

Only rarely do people report, with any confidence, memories of their earliest years. But your parents may be able to help you trigger some. Here are some questions you can use to interview your mother, and perhaps your father, about the early months and years of your life. The questions, and their answers, will probably prompt your own recollections and feelings as well as your parents'. Here are some guidelines for conducting an early life interview:

Some Interview Guidelines:

1. You can interview each parent separately or see them as a couple.

2. Bring a notebook and a tape recorder, if everyone is agreeable. Notice what's going on inside your head as you ask the questions and hear your parents' answers. Try to capture that also.

3. The list of questions is not sacred; add to or subtract from the questions as you proceed.

4. If you do tape-record the interview, you may trigger other memories and interpretations of your parents' answers when you replay the tape.

5. When your memories or your parents' don't relate to the early years of your life, or to the specific question, capture and explore them anyway.

6. While these questions are phrased to be asked of your mother, you can easily adapt them to a father, grandparent or relative. Again, the questions are merely guidelines; modify them anyway you like.

Questions About Pregnancy

What was it like for you when you were carrying me in your womb? (And what was it like for father?)

What kind of food did you eat? Did you have any favorites? Was any food really repulsive to you?

Were you smoking at the time?

Did you take any medication while you were carrying me?

What did you notice about me in the womb? Did I move around a lot, kick much, or was I still?

Were you well physically during the pregnancy? Temperamentally, were you excited? Calm? Anxious? How did my father behave?

About Birth

Where was the delivery? In the hospital? At home?

How long were you in labor altogether? What was it like?

Was it a natural birth or section? Were drugs used?

Who was with you during delivery? What else do you remember?

How long was it after birth before you got to see me? What was it like?

Where did I stay after birth (hospital nursery, your room, etc.)?

Was my father there during birth? What was it like for him and for you? If he wasn't there, when was the first time he saw me?

About the Early Months

Was I breast fed or bottle fed? On demand or on schedule?

If you nursed me, what was the nursing like?

_____

_____

_____

_____

_____

_____

_____

_____

_____

_____

_____

_____

_____

_____

_____

_____

_____

Did I have a separate room or stay with you or...?

How old was I when I was I weaned?

Did I have any illnesses or accidents during the first months?

Did I have any unusual weight gains or losses?

Did I eat well? Badly? What did I particularly like?

How long did it take for me to be toilet trained?

When did I learn to walk? Who helped me? What else do you remember about it?

About Early Childhood

Who held me a lot when I was young? You, father, the grandparents? Special friends? Anyone else?

What were my favorite toys?

What kind of personality did I have? How did you deal with me? Did I cry much? What were my sleep patterns like?

What did we do as a family that we all enjoyed?

Reading List

About the Nature of Memory

Schafer, Edith Nalle. *Our Remarkable Memory: understanding it * improving it * losing it?* Washington, D.C.: Starhill Press, 1992.

Elaborating and Preserving Memories

Fletcher, William. *Recording Your Family History: A Guide to Preserving Oral History Using Audio and Video Tape.* San Francisco: Ten Speed Press, 1989.

Goldberg, Natalie. *Writing Down the Bones: Freeing the Writer Within.* Boston, Shambhala, 1986.

Klauser, Henriette Anne. *Writing On Both Sides of the Brain: Breakthrough Techniques for People Who Write.* New York: Harper & Row, 1986.

Rainer, Tristine. *The New Diary: How to Use a Journal for Self-Guidance and Expanded Creativity.* Los Angeles: Tarcher, 1978.

Selling, Bernard. *In Your Own Voice:*

Using Life Stories to Develop Writing Skills. Alameda, CA.: Hunter House, 1994

Ueland, Brenda. *If You Want to Write: A Book about Art, Independence and Spirit.* St. Paul, MN: Graywolf Press, 1987. (1938).

Thorsheim, Howard L. & Bruce R. Roberts. *Reminiscing Together: Ways to Help Us Keep Mentally Fit as We Grow Older.* Minneapolis: CompCare Publishers, 1990.

Memory Computer Software

Family Tree Maker. Selective Software, 3004 Mission Street, Santa Cruz, CA 95060. 1-800-423-3556.

Memories! Senior Software Systems, 3103 Candlelight Court, Austin, TX 78758. 1-800-637-9949.
Offers interviewing and organizing techniques.

WritePro. 43 Linden Circle, Scarborough, NY 10510. 914-762-1255.
Primarily for writers of fiction.

Reading for Professionals

Memory and Remembering – Psychological Approaches:

Butler, Thomas (ed.) *Memory.* Oxford and New York: Basil Blackwell Ltd., 1989.

Neisser, Ulric. *Memory Observed: Remembering in Natural Contexts.*

San Francisco: W.H. Freeman, 1981.

Proust, Marcel. *Remembrance of Things Past.* New York: Vintage Books, 1982. (1913-1927).

Ross, Bruce M. *Remembering the Personal Past: Descriptions of Autobiographical Memory.* New York: Oxford University Press, 1991.

Rubin, David C. (ed.) *Autobiographical Memory.* Cambridge: Cambridge University Press, 1986.

Singer, Jefferson A. and Peter Salovey. *The Remembered Self: Emotion and Memory in Personality.* New York: The Free Press, 1993

Memory and Remembering: Philosophical Approaches:

Casey, Edward S. *Remembering: A Phenomenological Study.* Bloomington, Ind.: Indiana University Press, 1987

Warnock, Mary. *Memory.* London: Faber and Faber, 1987.

Sensation:

Ackerman, Diane. *A Natural History of the Senses.* New York: Random House, 1990.

Le Guerer, Annick. *Scent: The Mysterious and Essential Powers of Smell.* New York: Turtle Bay, 1992.

"The Intimate Sense of Smell," *National Geographic, September* 1986, pp. 324ff.; "The Smell Survey: Its Results," October 1987, pp. 514ff.

Communicating One's Memories:

Gibb, Jack R. *Trust: A New Vision of Human Relationships for Business, Education, and Personal Living.* North Hollywood: Newcastle Publishing, 1991.

Jourard, Sidney M. *The Transparent Self.* New York: Van Nostrand Reinhold, 1971.

Magee, James L. *A Professional's Guide to Older Adults' Life Review: Releasing the Peace Within.* Lexington, MA: Lexington Books, 1988.

Polster, Erving. *Every Person's Life is Worth a Novel.* New York: W.W. Norton, 1987.

Acknowledgements

Someone once asked William Saroyan how long it took him to finish *The Human Comedy*. He answered, "All my life." I know what he meant. During the decade-long nurturance of this work and myself, the only aspect for which I claim total responsibility (beyond its errors) is my persistence. In all other aspects I am indebted to many people—no one more than my wife, Joan H. Cole. Her imprint of warmth and brilliance may be found on many, many pages.

Richard Olney (1914-1993) was a master teacher and my mentor for the last ten years of his life. He encouraged this work, and understood the role of memory triggering in unblocking and stimulating the creative process. Dick encouraged my development of the book at each stage, even when I thought I might never complete it. When he died, my world was forever altered. I miss him, and I am deeply grateful for his many gifts of wit, of wisdom and of poetry. He was a man of special distinction. I wish that he were here to read this final product.

Among others I would like to thank specifically: Joan Minninger for showing me, in the writing workshops we conducted together, how memories could be triggered by commonplace objects. Bob Borson was my astute and gentle guide and editor through the first version of the manuscript; Kosta Bagakis carefully edited the final draft for bloopers. Helen Palmer, Laura Gans, and Kathryn Ridall saw clearly at the project's beginning those obstacles I then could not see at all. Dick Moore and Eric Greenleaf each offered their own kinds of personal support.

Participants in my workshops and in family experiments taught me what worked and what didn't. Bob Serrett and Karen Diasio Serrett, David Wendlinger, Peter H. Cole, Alan Lakein, Michael Feinstein, Jim Meltzer, Suzanne

Slyman, Anngwyn St. Just, Leslye Russell and John Larson, Jeffrey Klein, Paula Bodenstein, Marcia Perlstein, Roz Parenti, Emily and Morris Schaffner, and Miriam and Erving Polster offered support in other ways, commenting perceptively either on the process or on various drafts of the manuscript, and sometimes on both.

I also want to thank, for contributing their early life-stories to these pages: Susan Haynes Borson, Ann Collentine, Carolyn Reid-Green, Suzanne Rubel, Marta Wendlinger, Marcella Kenny, and (again) Mr. Borson and Ms. St. Just.

A Familial Note

To my three children—David, Marcella and Marta: This book was inspired by my determination not to repeat with you the legacy of mystery and silence left to me by my father. Though he was a loving man, his inaccessibility and my shyness converged to keep us from truly knowing one another. I wanted this not to be so with my own family. So as triggering taught me (unexpectedly) more about my father, I hope that this book has shown you parts of me— some subtle, some dramatic; some probably known to you, some only vaguely familiar, and some surely mundane—which may surprise you, please you, and perhaps motivate you to seek more memories of your own.

I think the triggering process has the potential of becoming a powerful multi-generational game, using the stories of our lives as material, with further closeness and intimacy as the result—so everybody wins. I hope you will someday use this book with me, with each other, and with your families and children. Someday perhaps my grandson Scott will trigger memories with his parents, becoming interested in some of their stories before he was born and in those other stories that they have created together as a family.

Joan's three sons and their families also have a special place in my heart. You have shared your worlds and your lives with me so openly that you have become my beloved family during the past eleven years. As with my own children, your interest in this book, even when you possibly wondered if it would really happen, both prodded and supported me.

Credits

19, 157	From the garage of Marcella Kenny
25, 29, 45	Courtesy of Mrs. Hazel Borson, Minneota, MN
37	Collection of Robert I. Wendlinger, Eastchester, NY
41	Noxzema ® The Procter&Gamble Company. Used with permission.
97	Courtesy of Jonah Klein, Berkeley, CA
135	Ivory Soap ® The Procter&Gamble Company. Used with permission.
169	Collection of Harriet and Alden Getz
171	Snow dome collection of Shelley Spicer and David Wendlinger

Recordings:

27	*Billboard Greatest Christmas Hits, 1955–Present.* Rhino R2 70636.
53	*Television's Greatest Hits 70s and 80s.* TVT 1300 CD. (TeeVee Toons Inc., 23 East 4th St., New York, N.Y. 10003.)
87	*Songs That Got Us Through WWII.* Rhino R2 70960.
147	The Beatles. *Sgt. Pepper's Lonely Hearts Club Band.* Parlophone CDP 7 464422.
155	*The Jack Benny Show: Two Radio Broadcasts.* Radio Yesteryear/Radiola Records. CDMR #1147. (Box C, Sandy Hook, CT 06482.)

I would also like to thank my 386SX (modified), Spellbinder, PC-Outline, ZyIndex and Word Perfect (4.2, 5.0, 5.1, and 5.1+) for their assistance in the completion of this project.

Bob Wendlinger, developer of the Memory Triggering Process, has had a successful career in the fields of organizational and interpersonal communications. He directed worldwide internal communications at the world's largest bank, co-authored a well-known college textbook on business writing, and contributed chapters on communication and supervision to several books, including the McGraw-Hill *Encyclopedia of Professional Management.* He has also been an adjunct professor in the MBA program at St. Mary's College in Moraga, California. He is married to Dr. Joan Cole, and they have six children and four grandchildren between them.

The Proust Press offers publications and other products of interest to those who wish to recapture their memories. These include Memory Triggering Workshops, audio tapes, and interactive computer software for memory triggering. Your memories and your comments for the next edition will be welcomed. Please contact:

Proust Press
6239 College Ave., #303
Oakland, CA 94618
Telephone 510-845-5551
CompuServe: 73151,1702